Create
your
own
graphic
design
portfolio
online
and in
print

Winning Portfolios
for Graphic Designers

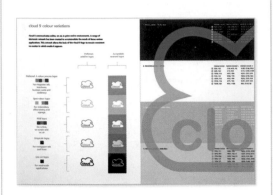

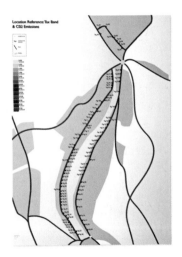

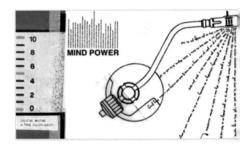

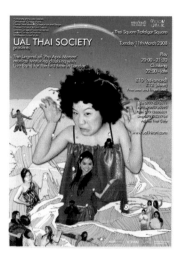

Create
your
own
graphic
design
portfolio
online
and in
print

Winning Portfolios

for Graphic Designers

Cath Caldwell

Introduction   6
About this book   6
10 Pointers for a perfect portfolio   8

1 PREPARATION

Planning your portfolio   12
Print vs. digital   16
Size and shape   18

2 EDITING YOUR ARCHIVE

Portfolio: Design agency   22
Digital portfolio: Design agency   30

Portfolio: Design studio   32
Digital portfolio: Design studio   40

Portfolio: Packaging design   42
Digital portfolio: Packaging design   50

Portfolio: Brand design   52
Digital portfolio: Brand design   60

Portfolio: Advertising   62
Digital portfolio: Advertising   70

Portfolio: Book design   72
Digital portfolio: Book design   80

Portfolio: Magazine design   82
Digital portfolio: Magazine design   90

First edition for North America published in 2010 by Barron's Educational Series, Inc.

A QUARTO BOOK

Copyright © 2010 Quarto Inc.

3 DESIGN FOR ONLINE PROMOTION by Chris Jones

Portfolio: Online	94
Portfolio: Website	102
Portfolio: Blog	106
Portfolio: Network	110
Choosing and using templates	114
Get your portfolio noticed	116
Creating a one-page presence	117

4 PROMOTING YOURSELF

Writing your résumé	120
Designing your résumé	123
Writing your cover letter	126
Starting your own business	130
Searching for jobs	132
The interview process	134
Promotional ideas	136
Resources	140
Index	142
Credits	144

All inquiries should be addressed to:
Barron's Educational Series, Inc.
250 Wireless Boulevard
Hauppauge, New York 11788
www.barronseduc.com

ISBN-13: 978-0-7641-4505-6
ISBN-10: 0-7641-4505-3

Library of Congress Control No.:
2010924476

QUAR.JSS

Conceived, designed, and
produced by
Quarto Publishing plc
The Old Brewery
6 Blundell Street
London
N7 9BH

Senior editor: Katie Crous
Copy editor: Karolin Thomas
Art director: Caroline Guest
Art editor and designer:
Jacqueline Palmer
Picture research: Sarah Bell
Photographers: Phil Wilkins and
Simon Pask
Creative director: Moira Clinch
Publisher: Paul Carslake

Color separation by PICA Digital
Pte Ltd., Singapore
Printed in Singapore by Star
Standard Pte Ltd.

10 9 8 7 6 5 4 3 2 1

The purpose of this book is to help you represent yourself. As a graphic designer you may have particular skills, but when it comes to showing this talent you may need a little encouragement. This book should enable you to see your work as others do.

I have selected real portfolios from students, graduates, and young freelancers to show the huge variety in content and format available. You will pick up practical tips while being inspired by great ideas in the pages to come.

Think of your portfolio as a work in progress. Regard it as a fluid record, to be adapted and changed for almost every interview. It is a reflection of who you are and what you are capable of. As you enter the creative work environment, this book will equip you with the knowledge of how to adapt your work to suit the various fields of design, and prepare you for a challenging career.

Cath Caldwell

About this book

Split into four chapters, the book starts with a general guide to portfolios, then examines exemplary, real student portfolios in detail before moving on to an informative digital section and ending with a special section on searching and applying for jobs.

Chapter 1: Preparation

A guide through the preliminary and key aspects of choosing the presentation style and format of your portfolio.

Chapter 2: Editing your archive

The main bulk of the book examines different disciplines in the graphic design industry and shows you how to meet the relevant criteria for getting a job in each one, through the successful selection and presentation of your work. Each discipline is organized into the sections shown opposite.

Chapter 3: Design for online promotion

This section identifies the various options available for putting your portfolio online, and getting it noticed (see example opposite).

Chapter 4: Promoting yourself

Indispensable advice on finding and applying for jobs or starting up on your own.

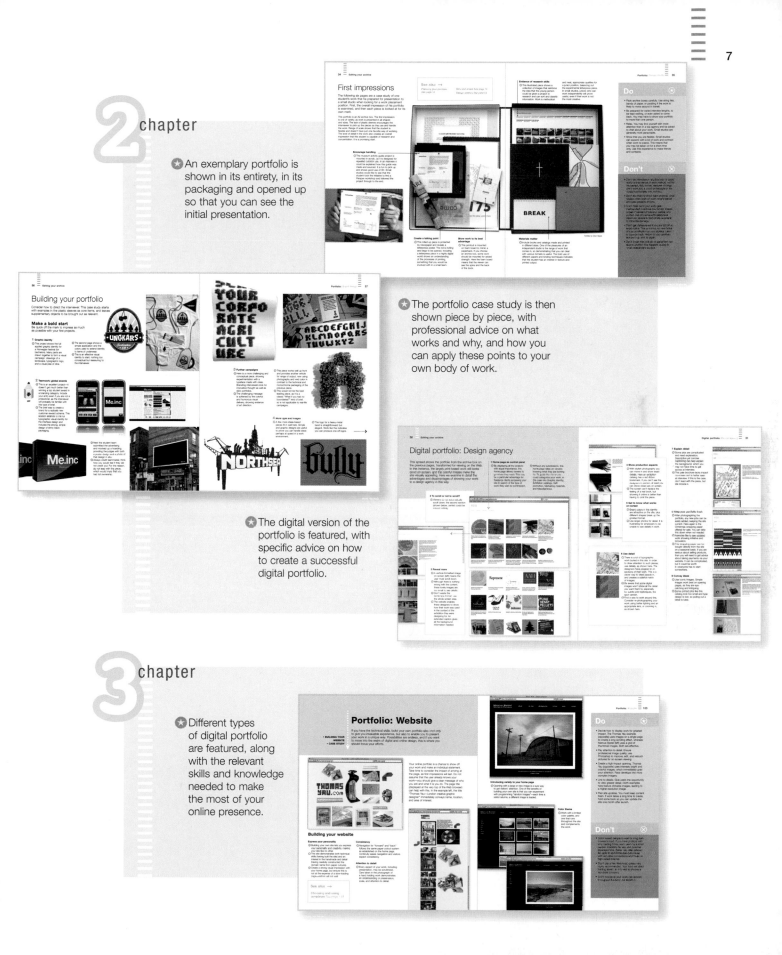

chapter 2

⭐ An exemplary portfolio is shown in its entirety, in its packaging and opened up so that you can see the initial presentation.

⭐ The portfolio case study is then shown piece by piece, with professional advice on what works and why, and how you can apply these points to your own body of work.

⭐ The digital version of the portfolio is featured, with specific advice on how to create a successful digital portfolio.

chapter 3

⭐ Different types of digital portfolio are featured, along with the relevant skills and knowledge needed to make the most of your online presence.

10 Pointers for a perfect portfolio

1 Don't take a portfolio and lots of plastic bags with other material in; it just looks unprofessional. If you do have some 3D objects (such as the project shown above), think carefully about taking one extra bag only.

2 You don't need to show more than ten pieces. If you can't demonstrate your talents in that number, there may be inherent problems with the quality of your work.

3 Remember your interviewer will be taking time out of a busy schedule, so a bulging portfolio is not encouraging to look at, and may be memorable only for its thickness.

4 Let interviewers turn the portfolio pages at their own speed. It can be irritating to them and not beneficial to you if you hang on to a page and start telling long-winded anecdotes about particular pieces that they might think irrelevant or simply not like.

5 Remember typefaces and photographers' names. It is not very convincing that you worked on a piece if you can't remember important design details.

6 Remember the logistics of how you created each of your portfolio pieces. Your potential employer will be looking for evidence of planning, working methods, and the ability to hit schedules.

7 Look at the company website before you go and see if there is anything you can show from your archive to demonstrate the relevant skills (or be aware that you may need further training on the job).

Representing yourself in a portfolio is a rewarding exercise, and gives you a chance to reflect on your work. Your portfolio should tell the story of your skills and strengths and define who you want to be.

You may get an interview by sending samples of work as a PDF or via your website, but almost all employers will want to meet you and see some of your printed work before employing you.

8 Maximize the time you have to present your portfolio by not being late. Aim to get there thirty minutes early just in case; there is nothing more unsettling for you than arriving sweating and with a head full of excuses.

9 Don't put personal drawings and early brainstorming sketches into the body of a finished portfolio, unless you know for sure that the client is interested in seeing this type of work.

10 Don't put your work in chronological order the way you might be asked to do for a college assessment. The client wants you to sort your portfolio into a logical sequence that shows your work off to its best advantage.

How perfect is perfect?

Your work need not be perfect—it just has to be the best you can do for now. Don't worry too much; instead, direct your energy into producing strong content, and relax and prepare for the interview. Don't stay up all night mounting work and arrive the next day stressed out. Your portfolio will grow with you: You will add to it and remove old pieces as often as you change hairstyles. No one expects more from a graduate portfolio, so don't fret if it does not look professional enough. With a few years' experience, you will return to it, improve it, and see it through different eyes.

Take criticism

If your field is advertising, you will quickly get used to the idea of a portfolio as a tool for critical feedback. One person may like a campaign and another may dislike it. Stand firm and don't worry. If your field is interactive design, feedback may arrive in blogs. Don't overreact to one person's critical feedback, especially if that person is a competitor!

The digital world

You may be surprised at how many people click on your digital portfolio, but are they the right people? Your work may elicit many browsers, but you may not get job offers without contacting employers. There are now millions of portfolios online; this book will help ensure that yours is in the right place, at the right time, and is edited to stand out from the crowd. See Design for online promotion, page 92.

preparation

Before you start selecting work for your portfolio, it is vital that you give some thought to how it can best be presented. Over the following pages, familiarize yourself with the various devices and tactics available to you: mounting work to give it a professional look, for example; or keeping your portfolio neat and the work within it undamaged by packing it correctly. Captions and page headings can be used for clarity and cohesion, but observe the spell-check rule: check, then check again.

Throughout this book, both print and digital portfolios are addressed. The sanctity of print remains prevalent in the graphic design industry, but it does so alongside the dominance of digital. You should embrace both formats for your portfolio, but know which one will work best for you in any given circumstance. The comparison in this chapter will help you to understand the benefits of each, and will lead you to make informed decisions.

chapter

1

The portfolio itself is second to the
work within it, but it needs to unify and
complement your collection of work.
So although the size and shape of your
portfolio may depend to some degree on
the content and on the field in which you
wish to gain employment or experience,
read up on the advantages and pitfalls of
the options available to you before you
make your choice.

Planning your portfolio

Build a portfolio to reflect what you can do both now and, more importantly, in the future. Planning is about telling your story in your absence. It involves turning a loose set of projects, self-generated or from college, into a cohesive collection.

No matter the content or aim of your portfolio, there are some key aspects to consider when putting it together.

1 Keep presentation tidy

Keep presentation neat, but not so neat that it is stripped of any personality. Again, the nature of your work will dictate the overall presentation. Use rulers, metal straight edges, and sharp cutting blades for best results when compiling your portfolio.

Bound together

⭐ This undergraduate portfolio has many components, gathered together in an A3 binder.

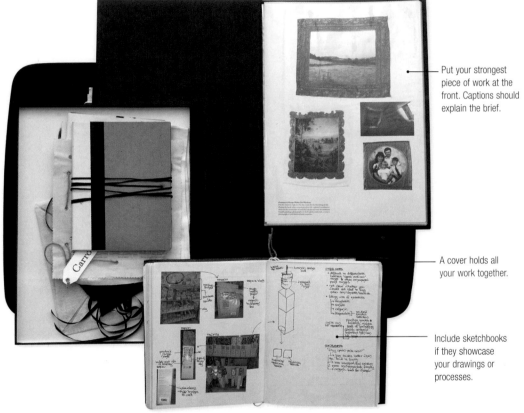

Put your strongest piece of work at the front. Captions should explain the brief.

A cover holds all your work together.

Include sketchbooks if they showcase your drawings or processes.

2 Mount work

Consistent presentation is paramount. Work tends to look better framed, although an attractive mount won't improve a poor piece. Focus on content: Look at detailing of type, finishing off layout, and printing to the best standard possible.

Lay pieces on colored paper. Avoid heavy card—this makes your portfolio too heavy. Don't always use black or white; instead, consider a neutral color, such as dove gray, to set off book page layouts. You can switch colors midway through; there's no need to stick to black if you started with it. Just do what looks best.

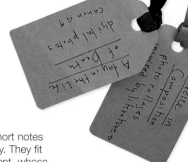

Tag it

⭐ These tags contain short notes and are fun and quirky. They fit perfectly for this student, whose interests are fashion and graphic design. Here the portfolio form originates from the function—a passion for clothes, art direction, and labels.

3 Caption carefully

Think of a signage system. It needs to explain work in the fewest possible words. Captions must be clear and easy to read, not an eye test or puzzle. This should be second nature, but graphic designers often omit captions, assuming mistakenly that viewers have previous knowledge of projects. Here are a few examples of caption methods (see also the portfolios in Chapter 2 for further examples).

Caption format

⭐ Captions can be mounted on card and clipped or lightly adhered to work. This is useful for packaging projects not mounted inside a plastic sleeve. Short descriptions give enough background to contextualize the piece, and further information is provided in expanded captions on the website.

Brand Heroin

The project illustrates how people can be addicted to consumption of certain goods by using a metaphor from a Romance novel.

"You are exactly my brand of heroin" is a quote which has been extracted from the Romance novel by Stephenie Meyer, Twilight (2006).

Media & the Ideal Happiness

The project explores the meaning of ideal happiness in relation to media and the

The book compares the ideal world power in Hello magazine [no ideal happiness (love) in [fiction]. Hello magazi perception and m happiness lies this is not n is very fra

Child Sweatshop

The photographs aim to raise awareness about the child sweatshop project suc

The project explores the significance of time in realtion to the definition of luxury. have

The wa

PRISM

Branding and designing packaging for a tea cocktail drink. The brand, PRISM, means spectrum of colour. It represents the colour change during the diffusion of tea.

The written word

Take greatest care with typography, and don't forget spelling—use a spell-check. Stick to black text; avoid gray or pastel colors that are hard to read. If you want to use white text reversed out of black, then be careful to make sure it is legible. Choose fonts that are not too fine so that they hold up (and don't fill with black) when you print them. Aim for an exercise in simple beauty and clarity. Choose fonts designed for print on paper, not those designed to be read on-screen, for example, Courier or Arial. If you don't know the difference, do some research (see Ellen Lupton's Thinking With Type site http://www.papress.com/thinkingwithtype/letter/screen_fonts.htm).

Headers

⭐ A short heading running across the top might be a solution for explaining the context of your work. This device would be effective for branding or advertising portfolios.

From academic to professional

When you leave college your assignments may look perfect for academic assessment, but you need to consider the point of view of an interviewer. If they have seen many portfolios, then the likelihood is that they have seen similar assignments. Therefore, you need to push your work to a more professional level. Consider reprinting assignments with a higher quality of production and presenting them in an original way.

A running head can be a useful categorizing and contextual tool.

4 Pack with care

Pack items carefully so they don't rattle around. Some students choose archive boxes; however, you may find that these leave a lot of empty space. In transit, use a device or padding to hold pieces in place.

Crafty solutions

🚫 An A5 book cover is floating around inside this large, flat C2 archive box. If sending such a box by courier, the solution is to build a jig—a frame containing holes into which smaller work fits. Here the large flat box is opened to reveal A3 posters held by a white band. The smaller books fit neatly into slots cut from ⅕ in. (5mm) foam board. On removing the jig, A2 work is revealed.

Jig cut out of polyboard/foam board.

The jig is put in place and the items are held in the allocated windows.

A paper band is slipped around A3 posters and holds them together.

5 Love at first sight

First impressions are always vital, and what to put on the first page is a tough choice that you may never have previously considered. While an interview progresses, the page may be left open, so it must be memorable.

Optional name

⭐ You could put your name on the top page, in a stylish way to reflect your current tastes.

Compare your options

⭐ Opening pages can make a significant difference. Choose something bold with a brave use of scale. Here two options show that the big mouse head is a stronger lead as it is bolder and more confident than the piece on the left—a detailed illustrated story. The mouse is memorable as part of a fanzine project for this illustrator/designer.

Be clever

⭐ In case this portfolio is mistakenly viewed from the back, so the carefully selected front page is not showing, the joke message "I'm upside down, please turn me over" still impresses the viewer, with a bright idea. Imitating the base of a cardboard box, the page presents an everyday object in an unusual way—perfect for an advertising student to demonstrate that form and function are unified.

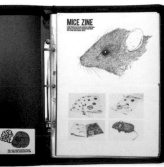

Divide it up

⭐ These A2 sheets (divider pages, not captions as such) categorize loose sheets of work. Again, signage reflects portfolio content. An interest in letterforms is key, and translucent material reflects a love of print processes.

Packaging 3D

⭐ The individual 3D items of this packaging portfolio are safely contained in corrugated cardboard boxes. Containers are labeled so that the interviewer can replace projects into the right boxes.

Do ✪

- Make sure your portfolio tells a story in your absence. Signage should be clear and concise. It should lead the viewer from start to finish in the way that a book designer takes a reader through a book from front page to back.

- Start with something memorable, provide solid content in the middle, and finish with a bang. Don't leave your best piece until last; particularly in advertising and branding, put your stellar work right up front.

- Use a bag or a folder. Even an archive box needs some kind of cover, so consider the logistics.

Don't ✗

- Don't forget to name your portfolio. You would be surprised how many A2 portfolios look just the same. Put your name on the outside so that it is never mistaken for anyone else's.

- Don't lose your portfolio. Keep it safe when at college or in a coffee bar. It could be stolen both for the work and for the case itself. Put a permanent note inside with your name, address, and return details. Keep copies of pieces in case you need to build a duplicate.

- Don't keep lots of empty blank sleeves in the back of the binder. This makes your portfolio unnecessarily heavy, gives a false impression of its fullness, and makes it look unfinished.

- Don't use the portfolio for storing magazines, a ruler, or a pencil case. Your portfolio should contain only what the interviewer needs to see.

Print vs. digital

Which is the better option for presenting your portfolio, print or digital? The answer lies in content of work and choice of employment. The reality is that you will have to create pieces in both print and digital format.

Designers like to see, touch, and hold items and projects such as glossy magazines, printed books, and packaging—it is in their nature to enjoy these things. Interviews in the art and design sector differ from panel situations in other professions—interviewers may well want to view both your site and your physical portfolio. We all love the digital images that fill our world, but there is a tactile side to graphic design that remains prevalent. Paper, card, and packaging are part of the communication process.

The drop-off

Bringing a portfolio for an appointment is an excuse to meet in person and have a conversation. However, you may be asked to drop off your portfolio instead—with an arrangement to pick it up later. Don't be surprised to have no contact with designers; you may have only a brief chat with a receptionist or junior designer, so remember, your work must speak for itself. Most agencies will contact you and confirm if they want to see you, but don't be afraid to ask for feedback if you were unsuccessful.

Print is best...

Q *What can you do in print but not on-screen?*

A See printed text in real size on real paper!

A Holding a printed book is an experience that connects hand and eye in a rewarding way. You can see text in relation to drawing, and experience cover texture. All these elements are part of the design solution, not just page layout.

A Pick up a piece of packaging, turn it over, and hold it in your hand.

A Portfolios won't crash or produce a 404 error!

A Include bookbinding projects, silk screen, and other book arts that need to be seen to be believed. The project on the left shows consideration for the reader and invites the viewer to put on gloves and experience the handmade item.

A Display pieces that are larger than a screen, especially useful for A2 posters. Who has an A3 screen to view work?

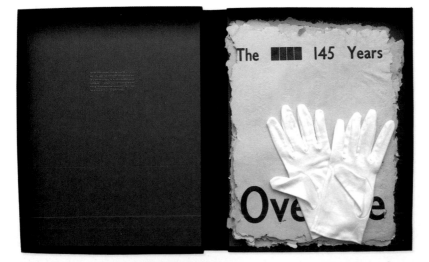

...No, digital is better!

Q *What can you do in a digital portfolio but not in print?*

A Send work anywhere in the world.

A Go public online for anyone to see.

A Update instantly on completing projects.

A Include extended research and backup work, more than in print.

A Add moving images and interactive work, and link to any such work you have posted on the Web.

A Photograph work in a way to look better on-screen than in a mocked-up version.

A Send work to specific people in other cities before you plan a trip. This saves time and energy.

A Link to a portfolio site where you are in a sea of other designers all looking for work (see Chapter 3).

A Track numbers of visitors who view your work week to week. You may have thousands of browsers.

A Save money on print and mailing costs.

A Use the many forms of social networking, such as Facebook and Twitter, to promote your work.

A Sell your work online, such as limited editions of screen prints.

A On a blog, you can show interests and activities. Be careful of embarrassing content!

A Unfold work if this is part of the design form. The letter above folds out to a poster.

A Add personality by packaging and labeling. Use creative labels and tags, and play with presentation to make your mark.

A Leave a gift when you go, such as a thank-you postcard or a business card.

A Appear in person. Interviewers look for designers they can work with; discussing your skills is a way to vet you, person to person.

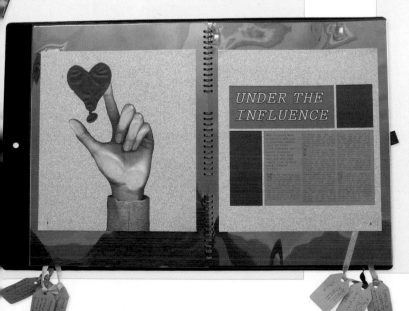

Size and shape

Content and type of industry determines presentation format. Examine work at length; reflection will help establish your strengths and weaknesses and where you would like to work. This will lead to choice in portfolio size and shape.

Don't buy a portfolio that is too big—work will look lost. As a rule, A1 portfolios are used for artwork—prints, drawings, and large-scale pieces—by fine artists and illustrators. The format is too impractical to take to graphic design interviews: few designers have desk space to open the folder. Arts students in general foundation courses often buy A1 portfolios for life drawings and large-scale experimental work; this is not appropriate for graphic designers.

A2 format

An A2 portfolio is a popular choice with aspiring designers. It is a large format for an interview so consider the logistics before investing.

▲ A neat fit

⭐ Many portfolios in this book are A2, a size that incorporates A3 books. Different projects fit nicely within this transparent case.

❗ You needn't spend a lot of money, but buy something solid. A plastic folder is a temporary fix, barely suitable for dropping off. It is not robust and will need replacing once it becomes scruffy.

◀ Consider a portfolio box

⭐ An A2 archive box is an expensive investment but could last a long time. Containing print work and A2 posters, it is used here to great effect. There is endless flexibility with such a box, adaptable for different interviews.

❗ A more traditional format may be more suited to a portfolio aimed at gaining work in the magazine or book design industries.

Where to buy portfolios

Bigger art suppliers stock portfolios. Photo stores have strong boxes. Book arts and bookbinding suppliers sell archive boxes with acid-free materials. You can even order a custom-made portfolio if you are not worried about budget. However, the quality of the work inside is more important than the quality outside—don't get so carried away packaging your work that you neglect the content.

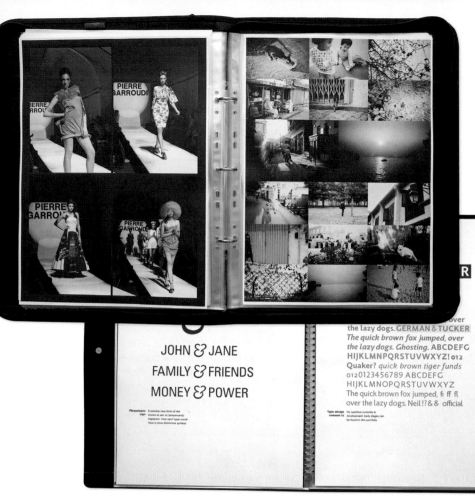

A3 format

An A3 portfolio with fixed sleeves gives complete control of a sequence. With a body of work to choose from, many accomplished designers leave an A2 portfolio at home and take selected pieces to different interviews in an A3 book or box.

◀ Ring-bound binders

⭐ This ring-bound format with loose sleeves means that the order of pieces can change between interviews without removing inner sheets; however, sleeves may eventually need renewal. If you drop the binder, rings may no longer align. At the back of this portfolio (top left) you can use pockets to store sketchbooks.

◀ Keep it simple and direct

⭐ For typographic pieces, A3 format allows the fonts to be presented clearly and captioned. Fixed pages (left) provide a smart alternative to the ringbound classic—the case is slimmer and they cost less.

▶ Packing a box

⭐ This box is slightly larger than A4, but work stacks easily inside. The graduates that use it, who have successfully started up their own business, have flexibility in an interview: they can retrieve the appropriate piece as the conversation develops.

A4 format

A4 boxes are popular with photographers and stocked at larger photography stores. To keep work clean and prevent rubbing, use acetate covers.

▲ Books for work experience

⭐ This simple, slim A4 portfolio with a caption at the top belongs to a student aiming for an internship, perhaps in magazines. Confident work focuses on photography with text; black and white is used because of budget restraints.

Avoid A5?

A5 portfolios are too small—interviewers want to see real-size typography, not shrunk down so that detail is lost. Don't waste time on miniatures.

editing
your archive

As a student, you will have amassed a body of projects from an academic environment. More vocational colleges may teach work-based elements and help initiate trade routes through internships. Many universities focus less on preparation for industry than on theoretical courses, exploring design as a form of communication. Therefore, your portfolio is probably a collection of academic pieces designed to pass assessments—a very different portfolio than one aimed at a design profession. What you need to do now is reevaluate and adapt academic study to practical experience.

This chapter examines how to edit different portfolios to show key skills and tell a personal story. You must edit an advertising portfolio—aiming for impact—in a different way than a magazine portfolio—needing an eye for detail. While it is possible to be a multi-talented designer with varied projects, in order to establish a career you need to present a style and approach aimed at a specific interest.

chapter

The following units focus on common types of employment to help determine what you may or may not want to do. Each path involves different approaches, even though all routes come under the general term "graphic design."

2

Portfolio: Design agency

- **KEY SKILLS**
- **FIRST IMPRESSIONS**
- **BUILDING YOUR PORTFOLIO**
- **DIGITAL PORTFOLIO**

Design consultancies look for portfolios that contain original and clear ideas. If you are aiming to get a job as a junior designer, remember this golden rule. Whereas design skills are no doubt required, creative thinking is paramount. Choose projects from your archive to show clearly that you are an ideas person who could add something new to an existing team.

What do design agencies do?

Most agencies produce branding, packaging, print, and other forms of communication. Design groups, consultancies, and agencies vary, but have a common thread: to shape society—what we read, touch, and use. Graphic designers solve problems and question why we need things in the first place.

Large design agencies tend to be stable, with a core staff in their offices, possibly in more than one location. However, it can be difficult for newcomers to find a way in. First consider getting some work experience at a smaller design group, before contacting one of the more famous agencies.

Pros and cons

⭐ Working for a large design agency can be exciting, with impressive client names.

⭐ Established design companies think big and may have offices in other countries. You may get the opportunity to work on global accounts or work abroad.

⭐ Another language may be an advantage to you, especially if clients are in the fashion or retail business.

❗ Design for online platforms is now a required skill, so if you regard yourself as exclusively a print designer, then you may be unsuccessful in securing employment.

Key skills a design agency looks for

Creativity: thinking outside the brief

⭐ This project is an appeal for funding for a degree show and is a classic example of original thinking. It combines a simple message in text with a surprise foldout poster to accompany the mailer. Design agencies look for original ideas and thinking that goes beyond the normal remit of graphic design.

Ideas, ideas, ideas

⭐ The sticky-tape identity shows a strong idea applicable to different marketing materials.
⭐ Agencies like direct, no-nonsense solutions to keep ideas simple.

⭐ Three-dimensional pieces are useful inclusions—they prove you are not confined to a computer but can think in three dimensions.

Strong graphics

⭐ Simple design ideas work best of all. Eye-catching pieces like these should form the basis of portfolios for design agencies, as they will make you stand out from the crowd and will leave a lasting impression.

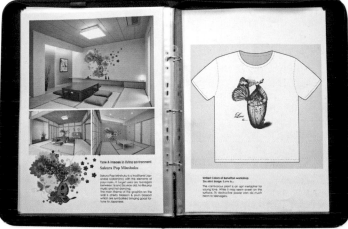

Skills and production values

⭐ A nicely structured book with sections shows a strategic and well-organized individual. There is clarity here with the left-hand page listing forthcoming work.

Long-lasting design solutions

⭐ This reusable Christmas card works like an internal office envelope, where the card is reused every year. It demonstrates that the designer understands that sustainable design solutions are all-important.

Motivation and character

⭐ Show low-tech skills and a willingness for hard work—agencies need nondigital thinking too. This piece took hours to make, reflecting a love of material and color. Everyone likes a junior who can cut and paste!

⭐ This piece suggests attention to detail and an eye for perfection—ideal character traits to convey through your work.

First impressions

This portfolio is ideal for presenting to a large design group. It contains graduate work along with some professional work. Your portfolio should show a talent for bright ideas displayed using a range of key design skills.

See also →

Planning your portfolio
See page 12
Size and shape See page 18
Design studio See page 32

Encourage handling

⭐ The hands-on nature of this box means the interviewer can pick up anything that may appeal instantly to him or her. It also works well if the interview is with more than one person, as others can join in and choose a book to look at.

Greater flexibility

⭐ This portfolio can be rearranged easily, unlike a fixed-sleeve portfolio. In this example, we show how the work can be reconfigured for a different design agency interview, with only printed work at the forefront. It is up to you to arrange the box appropriately for each presentation of your work.

Choose colorful work for impact

⭐ In this main photo the orange and green items pack a punch at the front, with the typographic work at the back.

❗ A few 3D pieces can sit at the front, but beware that they do not rattle around and cause rubbing. Instead, pack your portfolio properly to prepare for movement in transit.

Prepare for a drop-off scenario

❗ Sometimes you may have to leave your portfolio for the receptionist at the agency. Decisions about having loose 3D pieces to accompany the portfolio will have to be made. It is usually better if you can take your portfolio in person.

Portfolio by Ruth Sykes and Emily Wood

Do ⊛

- Be informed. Stand out from the crowd by being well prepared and knowledgeable about agencies, their work, and reputation. Prior knowledge creates a lasting impression.

- Tell agencies if you are a fan of particular pieces they have done and specifically why something inspired you. Saying, "It's nice" is okay; saying, "I like the reference to 1940s typography" is better. Show that you understand agencies' aims, and from their reputation what makes them different.

- Participate in design organization events and workshops. Take advantage of design community events using their websites, so you can still be a member without living in the locality.

- Get to know which agencies operate work placement programs and apply for them. Look in your local design press, online design news sites, and design annuals for competitions.

Don't ⊗

- Don't forget that agencies look for fresh creative thinkers to bring a new generation of ideas to the table. Show examples of problem-solving briefs and avoid purely decorative solutions.

- Don't forget skills. Once you have impressed agencies with your ideas, back this up with a few examples of typography.

- Don't assume that you will be taught everything once you arrive. Agencies require a basic standard so you can be left to work independently. In your résumé, include design software programs you know are needed. Try to find out minimum requirements.

Show typography skills

⊛ The printed examples contain a variety of fonts, used for different projects or freelance clients. The typography looks well developed and shows a flair for type and image, plus attention to small detail, all key characteristics for design agency work.

Show off…a little

⊛ Agencies look for people who participate in the design community, as they are informed and tend to stand out. Do say if you were short-listed in a student design competition (as was the example shown) or if you took part in a volunteer event as a helper. Mention the fact that you are a student member of a design organization or part of the design blog community.

Building your portfolio

If you want to work for a design agency, then edit your work down to flow from ideas-based projects to printed work that shows core design and production skills. In this portfolio we have edited the work into an ideal sequence. Using a loose box the sequence of work is variable, but here is one of the advisable ways to proceed.

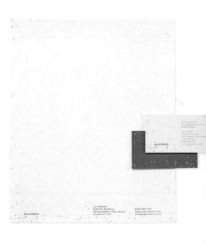

Starting your portfolio

This is the best place to demonstrate innovative thinking within a graphic design approach.

1 Lead with ideas-based work

⭐ Starting with these marketing materials for a portable exhibition illustrates a successful idea followed through to production. The visual elements here create a flexible identity, comprising color, shape, and the concept of using stickers and actual tape.

❗ Beware of identities that stamp the same logos repeatedly on items. This project shows that the designer understands that visual identity is about combining visual elements and an overall concept.

2 Include a branding project

⭐ This series of flyers for college short courses shows bold use of colors and graphic identity, which was developed for marketing purposes.

⭐ The flat colors indicate knowledge of print techniques, which is always good to see in a graduate portfolio. Even though you are not expected to be proficient at print, showing your basic knowledge of production is a strength.

⭐ The concept of the dotted line continues throughout these leaflets and provides a connection. Showing them all together gives impact.

3 Letterheads and business cards

⭐ Stationery items provide an opportunity to display good typography and strong branding.

❗ Don't lead with this, as its impact is not instant.

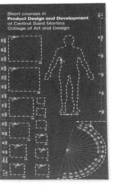

❗ In a presentation box, the subtle dotted-line visual link might be lost. Think carefully about how to show pieces that connect. Use your digital portfolio to reinforce your idea if needed.

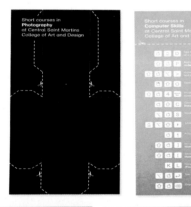

Pack a punch in the middle section

This is the best place to demonstrate design skills combined with ideas-based work.

6 Incorporating illustration

⭐ This annual report follows the previous piece but has a different feel and approach. Although the booklet appeared in the archive box, the open spreads demonstrate that the designer works well with illustration.

4 Color awareness

⭐ This freelance work, done after graduation, shows high production values. Make the most of any pieces like this, as they show that you can work within a professional context and that you can negotiate ideas with a reputable client, in this case a national museum.

⭐ Demonstrating knowledgeable use of Pantone colors, this invitation doubles as a coaster.

7 Toned-down pieces

⭐ By filling in this activity booklet, museum visitors can participate. At first, illustrations appear pale and without impact, so positioning them in the middle of the portfolio is best. This paces viewers' understanding to subtle levels of communication; not every piece needs to shout out.

5 Show you understand production values

⭐ This printed art exhibition catalog features the art pieces themselves in sparing layouts. The use of pictures in sequence conveys a sensitive handling of scale and pace on a page, and ribbon as a device for typography is a luxurious twist. This visually rich piece is for a fine-art audience and is high-end in its use of white space.

8 Show how your projects work

⭐ Both of these posters fold down into smaller booklets. They use simple, clever, and inexpensive print techniques.

❗ The posters are shown in the box as folded-up pieces, and the viewer may need encouragement to unfold them.

⭐ Designers like to see a body of text used in this way on a simple grid. It demonstrates typographic detailing and print skills.

9 Layout winner

⭐ This student project was a live project for a real client. The work was chosen as the winner in the student competition: include any such work as a talking point.

❗ You may have already covered layout booklet design in your portfolio. Consider editing this piece out if you are repeating yourself. Don't keep everything you have ever done; edit out duplicated points.

10 Personal work

⭐ The use of thermography and an ability to research cheery pastiche typography are both shown in this wedding invitation. Work that was obviously for friends is suitable for the portfolio initially, but should gradually be weeded out as your archive grows.

❗ Don't put small pieces like this at the very end, as your portfolio will tend to trail off; instead, tuck pieces in just before the end or omit.

Helpful hints

1. Make sure that you are clear about your requirements. What is most important to you: the cheapest ticket, the fastest journey or the flexibility to catch any train rather than being restricted? Let the ticket seller know this or you may not get the ticket most suited to your needs. For instance if you don't ask for the cheapest ticket

(except the Disabled Person's Railcard for which a special form can be obtained by writing to: Disabled Person's Railcard Office, PO Box 1YT, Newcastle, NE99 1YT).

Some form of identification may be required and, for a Young Person's Railcard, a passport-sized photograph will be needed. Most internet-based retailers do not sell Railcards.

31 ➡

At the particular desire of several Influential Persons

THE PARENTS & THEIR RESPECTIVE PARTNERS

Have the greatest pleasure to present

A MARRIAGE

Featuring Two Distinguished Personages whose Testimonials can be seen on application

EMILY and GEORGE

At the Residence known as

8 The Street, Berwick, East Sussex

parts of which will take place in a grand tent on a commodious piece of ground adjacent to the above abode

TO COMMENCE AT FIVE O'CLOCK

SATURDAY THE 2ND AUGUST

SEVERAL HOURS OF AMAZEMENT, WONDERMENT & DELIGHT!

including

A VEGETARIAN OPTION

regardless of expense. But excluding

THOSE LITTLE BAGS OF ALMONDS YOU ALWAYS LEAVE BEHIND

Have you heard the

SPLENDID BAND?

If not, come and hear it, and see Several Grand Allegorical Tableaux! Patrons are kindly asked to bring wellington boots and umbrella in case of rain falling on the betrothing couple in an entirely tasteful

HUMANIST CEREMONY

RSVP Emily & George, 57 Columbia Road, London E2 7RG
emily.wood@macmail.com/milton@macmail.com 020 7012 1209

The Committee of the Berwick Temperance Society regret that pets and children cannot be admitted for their own sake

Leave an impression

Include some memorable pieces of work at the end of your portfolio box so that you won't be forgotten once you leave the interview.

11 All-rounder

⭐ An all-round shining example of your skills is ideal for packing the end punch. This art exhibition catalog shows a high production standard, use of full color to create impact, and typography used in an evocative way.

⭐ This identity for an exhibition shows good use of pictures on a page, but is more of an editorial approach than an ideas-based approach. Keeping the display in creates great visual impact and makes a strong finish to the portfolio.

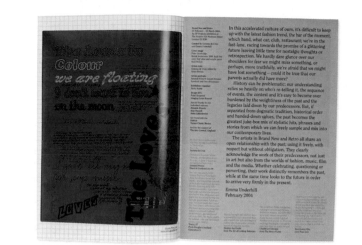

12 End with something memorable

⭐ This wrapping paper can be cut and reused as paper chains or as party hats. Simple and iconic, this piece shows evidence of graphic thinking. This kind of piece works well at the end, reinforcing strength in ideas.

⭐ This original work would benefit from being shown in 3D. The only way to do this would be to cut out and take one of the items folded. Otherwise you would have to direct an interviewer to your website to see a picture.

Digital portfolio: Design agency

This spread shows the portfolio from the archive box on the previous pages, transformed for viewing on the Web. In this instance, the largely print-based work still looks good on-screen, and the colorful images make the site visually appealing. Here we examine in detail the advantages and disadvantages of showing your work to a design agency in this way.

1 Home page as control panel

- By displaying all the projects with equal importance, this home page allows viewers to go where they want. This may be a particular advantage for freelance clients accessing your site in search of the type of work they wish to commission.

- Without any subdivisions, this home page relies on viewers knowing what they are looking for. To guide the viewer you could categorize your work, in this case into Graphic identity, Exhibition catalogs, Self-promotion, Marketing materials, and Miscellaneous.

2 To scroll or not to scroll?

- Viewers do not automatically scroll down; the second section (shown below, center) could be missed entirely.

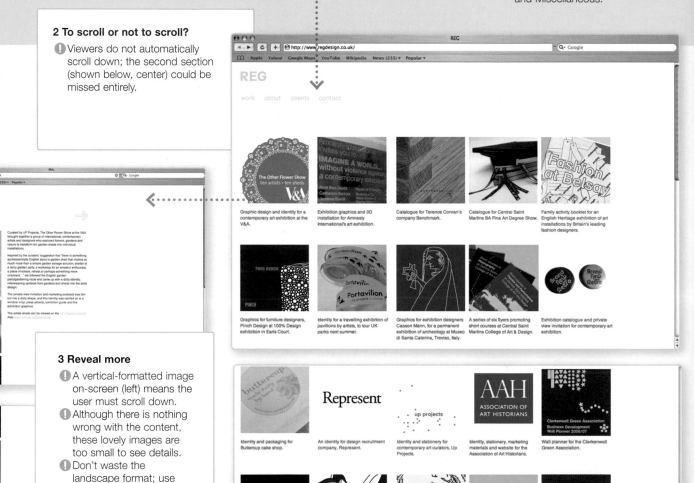

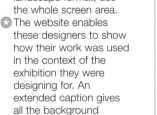

3 Reveal more

- A vertical-formatted image on-screen (left) means the user must scroll down.
- Although there is nothing wrong with the content, these lovely images are too small to see details.
- Don't waste the landscape format; use the whole screen area.
- The website enables these designers to show how their work was used in the context of the exhibition they were designing for. An extended caption gives all the background information needed.

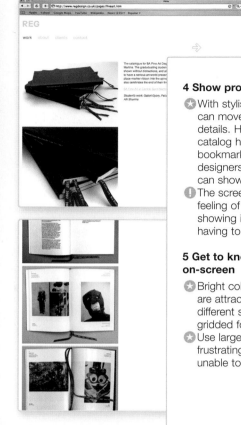

4 Show production aspects

⭐ With stylish photography you can move in and show exact details. Here an exhibition catalog has a red ribbon bookmark. If you can't see the designers in person, at least you can show close-ups on-screen.

❗ The screen can't replace the feeling of a real book, but showing it online is better than having to omit the piece.

5 Get to know what works on-screen

⭐ Bright colors in this identity are attractive on the site, plus different shapes break up the gridded format.

⭐ Use larger photos for detail. It is frustrating for employers to be unable to see details in work.

6 Use detail

⭐ There is a lot of typographic work buried in this site. In order to draw attention to such pieces, use details, as shown here. The designers have cropped in on sections of their work. This is a clever way to draw people in, and creates a colorful matrix of images.

❗ Be aware that some digital images won't show all the detail you want them to, especially for subtle print techniques, like spot varnish.

❗ Find a way to work around this. Consider re-photographing your work using better lighting and an appropriate lens, or zooming in, as shown here.

7 Explain detail

⭐ Some jobs are complicated and need explanation. Descriptive yet concise captioning can help explain the background, which you may not have time to get across at interview.

❗ This pale brochure lacks impact on-screen and is better seen at interview. If this is the case, don't lead with the piece, but still include it.

8 Keep your portfolio fresh

⭐ After photographing the portfolio, any new jobs can be easily added, keeping the site current. Here again is the Christmas wrapping paper offered for sale. You can take this down when not needed.

⭐ Agencies like to see updated work showing initiative and innovation.

❗ This wrapping paper can be bought directly from the site on a seasonal basis. If you are serious about selling products, then you will need to get advice about taking payments via your website. It can be complicated, but it could be worth it—everyone has to start somewhere.

9 Convey ideas

⭐ Use iconic images. Simple images work best on opening pages, as they are eye-catching and intriguing.

⭐ Some printed jobs like this catalog look too small and type design is lost, so pulling out a detail is ideal.

Portfolio: Design studio

- **KEY SKILLS**
- **FIRST IMPRESSIONS**
- **BUILDING YOUR PORTFOLIO**
- **DIGITAL PORTFOLIO**

Small design studios look for portfolios showing a range of skills plus evidence of personality in practice. Typically comprising five people or fewer working in proximity, studios want evidence that you can contribute to team projects and learn on the job. You will be expected to pitch in and will need good layout and typography basics.

What do design studios do?

Most city studios are small businesses employing fewer than five people in one room. Small studios offer exciting opportunities and are an ideal place for work experience. Be ready for anything—from making coffee to detailed typographic design. Dress smartly—a client may walk in or you may be asked to help at a presentation. If you are looking for a job in a small studio, be prepared for a variety of reactions to your work.

Independent studios often don't advertise for new designers. Instead they use word of mouth and trust the recommendations of their community of designers. Get involved by securing some unpaid work experience while you are in college.

Key skills a design studio looks for

Hands-on approach

⭐ Smaller studios may work on crafted one-off pieces. This hand-cut type is quirky and interesting. Studios look for unique designers who offer different takes on the world; put something handmade in your portfolio.

Pros and cons

⭐ Communication and negotiation skills develop in a small environment.

⭐ Many graduates start somewhere small to gain experience and to learn the jargon of graphic design before moving on to a larger agency. Getting paid work can be hard, however, so try to gain an internship.

⭐ The atmosphere is often more comfortable than at an established agency.

❗ If you prefer to work alone and don't take criticism well, you will have to learn to listen and accept feedback.

❗ If you are a specialist and keen to develop one particular skill only, consider other options than the varied design-studio life.

⭐ This example shows two students working on a project using hand-cut letters. They have obviously spent a lot of time preparing for this shoot. The low-cost nature of this is appealing, as small studios run on lower budgets than larger agencies do.

Evidence of homework

⭐ This in-depth editorial project proves that the candidate can become immersed in a subject. As the junior on a team, you might research a project or look into pricing suppliers.

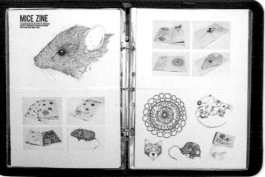

⭐ Before editing your portfolio for interview, take a look at what kind of work the studio specializes in. Here the designer has included drawings made and used in the context of a fanzine. Using work of the type that you know the studio produces could provide a common link, or at least a talking point in the interview.

Originality

⭐ Small studios have a variety of clients and can often be individualistic in their approach. Be yourself and show what you like to do. This portfolio includes posters, book covers, and lots of colorful paper cut-out ideas. It is unconventional and is not corporate oriented.

⭐ Often small studios have broken away from the corporate design environment and set up by themselves to enjoy more control over their work. The fees are smaller, but the work is less bureaucratic and aims for highly original outcomes.

Team player

⭐ Designers who demonstrate they can fit into a team will do well. This photo shows a collaborative project in which the two students prepared a life-sized children's race based on an analysis of children's gaming activity. They built props together and organized a real race, which they filmed and photographed.

First impressions

The following six pages are a case study of one student's work that he prepared for presentation to a small studio when looking for a work placement position. First, the overall impression of his portfolio is examined, and then each piece is looked at for its own merit.

This portfolio is an A2 archive box. The first impression is one of variety, as work is presented in all shapes and sizes. The lack of plastic sleeves encourages the interviewer to pick up the pieces as they are and handle the work. Range of scale shows that the student is flexible and doesn't have just one favorite way of working. The level of detail in the work also creates an overall impression that this student is capable of research and concentration. It is a promising start.

See also →

Planning your portfolio
See page 12

Size and shape See page 18
Design agency See page 22

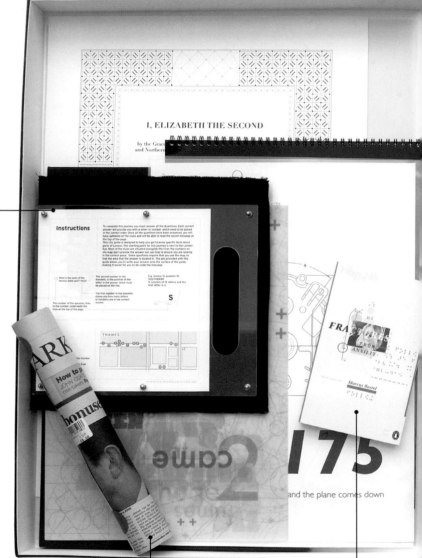

Encourage handling

⭐ This museum activity guide project is mounted in acrylic, as it is designed for repeated outdoor use. In an interview it could be explained how this guide was made and sourced. It is fun to pick up and shows good use of 3D. Small studios would like to see that the student took the initiative to find a Perspex workshop and followed the project through to the end.

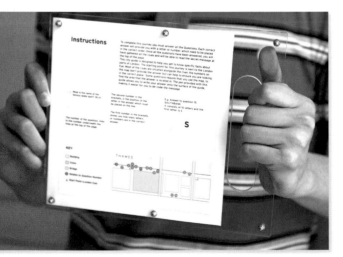

Create a talking point

⭐ This rolled-up piece is protected by newspaper and reveals a letterpress poster. The roll is inviting and begs to be opened. Including a letterpress piece in a highly digital world shows an understanding of the processes of printing, something that you would be involved with in a small team.

Show work to its best advantage

⭐ This printout is mounted on foam board to mimic a paperback. If you choose an archive box, some work should be mounted for added strength. Here the foam board means that the viewer can see the spine and the back of the book.

Evidence of research skills

⭐ This illustrated piece shows a collection of images that reinforce the idea that this young person could be given a project to research and can sort and classify information. Work is methodical and neat, appropriate qualities for a junior position, balancing out the experimental letterpress piece. In small studios, juniors who can work independently will prove useful, even if their work is not the most creative.

Portfolio by Oliver Mayes

Materials matter

⭐ Include books and catalogs made and printed in different sizes. One of the pleasures of an independent studio is the range of work that comes in, so demonstrating that you can deal with various formats is useful. The bold use of different papers and binding techniques indicates that this student has an interest in texture and printed output.

Do ⭐

- Pack archive boxes carefully. Use string ties, bands of paper, or padding if the work is likely to move around in transit.

- Be prepared for varied interview lengths, to be kept waiting, or even asked to come back. You may have to show your portfolio to more than one person.

- Relax. You may find yourself with more attention than in a top agency and be asked to chat about your work. Small studios are generally more personable.

- Show that you are flexible. Small studios can expand with a lot of work and contract when work is scarce. This means that you may be taken on for a short time only. Use this experience to make friends and contacts.

Don't ⊗

- Don't be intimidated—studios look for basic ability and evidence of work method, not for the perfect, fully formed designer. If things don't work out, it could be because of the studio's personality mix, not you.

- Don't be afraid to show team projects; small studios often work on each other's pieces and pass projects around.

- Don't freak out if your work gets manhandled in archive-box format. Create copies if needed of precious pieces, and protect one-off pieces with cellophane slipcovers (available from photo suppliers) to minimize damage.

- Don't get disheartened if you are laid off at short notice. This is normal; no one thinks of it as a reflection on your abilities. Learn to bounce back. Return to your portfolio, spruce it up, and try again.

- Don't forget that one job or placement can lead to another; this happens quickly in small independent studios.

Building your portfolio

With an unfixed format like an archive box, you will probably put loose pieces on top. However, these four pages show an ideal sequence to follow when you are asked to present your work.

Lead with strong work first

Start off with your best work and let it make an impact within the first few moments of an interview. Don't save the best until last—put it at the front.

1 Show multiple skills

⭐ A strong piece that shows a number of skills is an ideal start. Inside the paper roll is this intriguing letterpress work. First, it displays an interest in typography and letterform. Second, it demonstrates know-how of color and print technique. Third, it was sold at a fanzine sale in a department store, so it crosses into handmade book territory.

3 Add a flash of color

✪ Make sure that you include some color pieces. This brown slipcase with two yellow books inside adds bright color to a largely black-and-white portfolio.

Book Design
Typography

2 Create sections

✪ Following the loose pieces in the top of the box, the student has printed out divider pages for use in a drop-off situation, to define the sections within the portfolio. Here the book design and typography section gives the opportunity to demonstrate relevant, industry-standard skills. (See panel, right, for more detail on divider pages.)

5 Competition entries

✪ This was a typographic solution to a competition brief set as extracurricular work. Although not the most colorful or dramatic section, the exercise has value, as it uses decorative typographic elements to create pattern in a certificate design for the Queen's Anniversary Prize for Higher and Further Education. The pattern references delicate engraved patterns that were traditionally used to mark a genuine certificate.

❗ The caption should say that this was extra work; it proves the student is prepared to put in extra effort and time. Students who enter competitions demonstrate motivation, even if they don't win.

4 Include book covers

✪ This is one of the simplest ways to show that you understand the connection between type and image. It is great to see book covers laid out properly with the bar code and spine type included, and a standard-size format used, as they look professional and convincing.

Vary work in the middle

Now that you've made an impact, keep up the pace with some in-depth and varied pieces.

6 Add a major project

⭐ As well as a Typography category, you could include a major project in its own section, particularly if this job took longer than others. Here is your chance to show favorite pieces of work.

⭐ Including a favorite piece is a golden opportunity to communicate your passion for your work as you talk about the piece.

Divider pages

Dividing your work into five categories should be sufficient. A suggested order is as follows:

1 Design projects
2 Typography and layout
3 Competition briefs and live projects
4 Research projects
5 Personal work

Alternatively:
1 Design briefs
2 Layout skills
3 Print-based work
4 Interactive
5 Other (or your own term, such as Miscellaneous, Personal projects, Freelance work)

For different studios you can vary and add work easily. Divider pages help viewers reconstruct your portfolio when they start to pack it away.

This archive box could get shuffled around in transit, as it is a large A2 format with smaller work within. By using the A2 divider pages, printed on transfer paper, sections are created to help the interviewer grasp the key points the designer is conveying in his portfolio. They also mirror the work, as transfer paper features in one of the pieces. Design your divider pages to complement the contents of your portfolio and to unify all the elements.

Grid Systems
Context

Tax Band: CO2 Emissions (g/km)

Band A: Up to 100	Band B: 101-110	Band C: 111-120	Band D: 121-130	Band E: 131-140	Band F: 141-150	Band G: 151-165	Band H: 166-175	Band I: 176-185	Band J: 186-200
Band K: 201-225	Band L: 226-255	Band M: Over 255							

7 Other skills

⭐ A category called Written studies could be included as an opportunity to reflect your research, classification, and writing skills.

8 Visual written pieces

⭐ Written work is more enticing if it is illustrated and designed, as this example shows.

❗ If your essay is just text on A4 paper, consider omitting it and showing another visual example of your research capabilities.

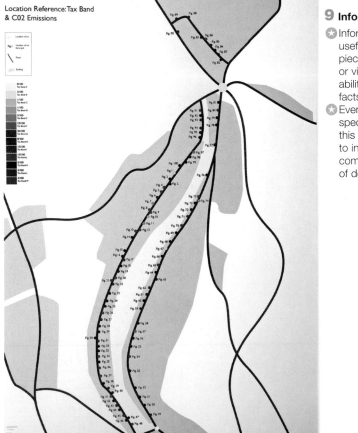

Location Reference: Tax Band & CO2 Emissions

9 Information design

⭐ Information design is often useful in a portfolio. Include pieces that may not be flashy or visual but demonstrate your ability to display graphically facts and figures.

⭐ Even if the studio does not specialize in information design, this would be a good piece to include because of the competent handling of a lot of detailed information.

OTHER

10 Create a miscellaneous section

⭐ The category Other is a "catchall" and useful when you reorder your portfolio. Add captions that tell which work is personal and which is college driven.

11 Experimental work

⭐ Experimental pieces can be a useful addition when it comes to showing off your creativity and ability to embellish standard forms.

❗ These decorative letters were part of a brief but need explanation to put them into context for the viewer. Some background information would be beneficial.

❗ If work is experimental, add a caption for clarity. Studio designers do not have time to quiz you on every piece.

REBIRD

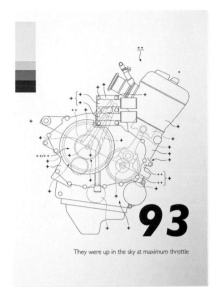

93

They were up in the sky at maximum throttle

175

They rise up, and the plane comes down

12 Graphic representation

⭐ By now you should have built up a rapport with the interviewer, and it may be the ideal time to show conceptual pieces that need further explanation about how they were generated. The pieces shown above are thoughtful and serious, developed from Martin Amis's article "What Will Survive of Us?" about the 9/11 terrorist attacks. They are an expressive graphic illustration of the airplane engines

❗ These extra pictures (right) are a development of the ideas above and are overprinted onto tracing paper. They could be omitted at a later date when more work builds up in this portfolio after graduation.

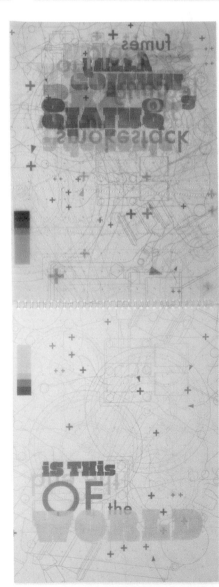

End confidently

Unify your portfolio by reasserting your professional interests and design values.

13 Reaffirm your style

⭐ A memorable piece will provide a suitable finish. This spiral-bound book returns to the core values of the student's interests. It uses strong copy and maximizes a bold typographic style to communicate a conceptual message in a simple and completed project.

IT IS EITHER
BLACK OR WHITE

A MAN SAYS TO ME
EVERYTHING I TELL
YOU IS A LIE
IS HE TELLING THE
TRUTH OR LYING

Digital portfolio: Design studio

One of the most effective ways to display work online is to transfer a typographic-based portfolio into a template, such as the WordPress site. Don't hesitate to present hand-printed work photographed in context, using concise captions. Small design studios want to see variety; they look for flexible people with a broad range of interests.

1 Make your profile page work

- The black background is strong. If printed out, the résumé strengthens impact: unexpectedly, it prints as black text on a white background. Remember that some employers may print, photocopy, or file your résumé.
- Clearer design could improve this profile page.

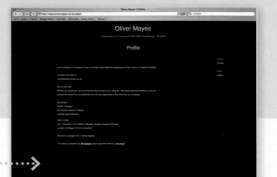

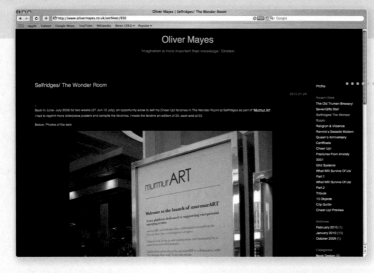

2 Contact details

- The name is centered at the top of the page; contact details are not yet inserted. Put your contact details next to your name or in another prominent place—no one wants to fish around looking for them.

3 Display high standards of presentation

- The letterpress fanzine in a zine sale is prominently positioned to give a very contemporary setting—a famous London department store.
- Viewers scroll down to see the display on the table. Not only is the work produced to a high standard, but the packaging of posters into paper tubes looks professional in this undergraduate portfolio.
- Selling pieces commercially brings the low-tech letterpress process into the business arena. Future employers will note that this student can produce work that relates to a buyer's market. If you have the opportunity to create something similar, photograph it and show it on your site.

4 Show typographic samples

- This competition entry is a detailed piece of typographic exploration using decorative characters; viewers can enlarge the image to see the detail. Make sure PDFs are correctly uploaded so they are not paneled once blown up. This is vital for typographic samples, as the screen devalues them, reducing A3 format to laptop size.

5 Repeat portfolio work

- Book covers, seen in the archive box on pages 34 and 36, reappear here for further scrutinizing. Interviewers may review work before or after interviews.

6 Use eye-catching images to convey ideas

⭐ Shooting a letterpress project in the print room gives a craft context and implies that the student is comfortable working in this area. A print technician holds the work; a caption details the background: "This was a self-initiated project that was completed in June 2009. The idea for the project came from seeing the newspaper headlines about the recession. I wanted people to cheer up!"

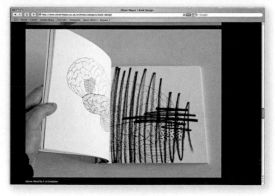

7 Show off book projects in 3D

⭐ Instead of photographing a book flat and closed, open it up to display the contents. You can do this easily to great effect, using your hands.

8 Include extra work

⭐ In the physical portfolio, the series of images may be edited down; on your website, include the full range.

⭐ The longer caption explains the research behind the visual outcome. Extend online information so that studios can return to your work in your absence and can ascertain your writing ability—a useful skill in a small team.

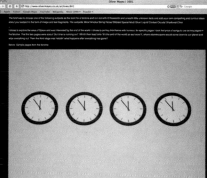

9 Put work into action

⭐ Indicate how a product is to be used. Here a wipe-clean Perspex tablet is the result of a signage brief, photographed in action to illustrate the piece in practice. Photographs can tell a story better than words.

11 Links to provide further insight

⭐ Showing things that interest you, through professionally relevant website links, contextualizes your work and gives insight into your personality. This student revealed the source of the photo below left—a shop specializing in twentieth-century art and design.

10 Add some personality

⭐ You probably collect items and visit places to build up a visual encyclopedia; refer to things that interest and inspire you. These photos, of a collection of graphic memorabilia, reflect an interest in type and information.

Portfolio: Packaging design

Packaging design agencies look for the magic combination of right-brain creative thinking plus left-brain logical thinking associated with neatness and organization; they want good ideas and strong problem-solving skills. Show your creativity in examples of new products designed to fill a gap in the market. Packaging is about understanding the consumer, so show solutions to briefs and evidence of your research process.

- **KEY SKILLS**
- **FIRST IMPRESSIONS**
- **BUILDING YOUR PORTFOLIO**
- **DIGITAL PORTFOLIO**

Key skills a packaging design agency looks for

Spatial awareness

⭐ Instead of taking 3D work with you, photograph it and produce neat layouts with explanatory captions to show you are an organized thinker. A standard A3 portfolio like this with fixed sleeves gives you control of the running order.

⭐ The opening page makes a strong statement about this young designer's priorities— she is interested in packaging first and foremost.

⭐ These portfolio pages show a 3D piece explained properly using photos shot in a studio. The professional lighting helps to show the work to its best advantage.

⭐ Hands in shots help show off small pieces, explaining how they should be viewed. This helps an interview go smoothly—potential employers can see both the actual piece and its use in context.

Award-winning creative work

⭐ Winning an international competition always looks impressive. Here the project— promoting fake textile windows for Antarctic explorers' tents—is a joint entry, demonstrating successful teamwork.

⭐ Don't be modest about your achievements. Flag them in your portfolio with captions and give a Web link in your résumé.

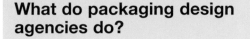

Creative thinking

⭐ There is a coordinated use of materials in this hand-bound A3 book (above). It shows research into paper quality and is an example of right-brain thinking.

⭐ The "gilded" items in the basket (right) demonstrate knowledge of product development. They take the subject of the essay in the A3 book above—the commercialization of shrines and cathedrals—even farther.

❗ The basket of paper goods is fragile, needing careful packing. In a drop-off situation, an interviewer may fear damaging it; a photograph may be preferable.

What do packaging design agencies do?

Packaging design companies develop identities for clients by helping to define the brand, what it does, and how the user experiences it. Designing the structure of the packaging and the graphic identity is only part of the process. Designers also work with existing brands to develop new product and packaging ideas to keep up with the changing marketplace. Finally, they work to improve the user experience by investigating paper, print processes, and environmentally sound packaging solutions.

Junior designers start by getting involved in making presentations and visualizing ideas, often working with a senior designer.

Understanding the packaging process

⭐ In an interview you can show your sketchbooks and mood boards. Here we see initial ideas in a sketchbook, with visual references, and the actual product, folded in the portfolio next to the work photographed and explained in the captions. Showing the whole process helps the interviewer see how you would work in the design studio.

Pros and cons

⭐ Packaging design is a dynamic field that keeps up-to-date with current trends and therefore is vibrant and exciting.

⭐ An interest in retail is important, as is a love of color, texture, and materials.

⭐ Increasingly, packages are presented to clients from all angles, so interactive designers interested in 3D drawing programs, and with advanced Photoshop skills, could find suitable employment in this sector.

⭐ Research is vital in this field. If you have designed a jar label, for instance, show that you have researched the marketplace, audited the category, and taken relevant photographs in-store.

❗ You will need a wide range of skills and to be able to see the big picture while also paying attention to the tiniest detail of a specification. If you don't like detail and accuracy, then avoid this area of graphic design.

First impressions

Presentations for packaging agencies involve demonstrating knowledge of 3D, often in flat artwork; mock-ups or models are not always practical. This case study shows different ways to use photography for presenting 3D work to best advantage, and how to choose which packaging projects to take and which to photograph.

See also →
Planning your portfolio See page 12
Size and shape See page 18

Pack your work for safety

⭐ This box contains loose work. In order to keep the work in a presentable condition you have to protect it; here the work is packed in small boxes, ready for transport. Labels help the interviewer repack it for you to collect. This is excellent practice, as it shows the care and respect for work that you will need in your career as a packaging designer.

Include 3D

⭐ Most packaging designers look at digital portfolios first so they can filter the right kind of candidates for interview. Therefore it is important to take some 3D items that cannot be experienced digitally. Holding something in your hand is critical, and illustrated boxes that can be opened up, like the ones pictured here, make the portfolio inviting.

Knowledge of branding

⭐ Packaging design is rarely a one-off product but more often an application of a graphic identity. Including an extension of a project, like this rubber stamp, which extends the brand identity of the Pack Green campaign book (also in box), demonstrates that you could apply an identity to different formats within one campaign.

Love of materials

⭐ This wooden box is sturdy and beautiful. Packaging studios are keen to see a love of material and textures, so a box like this would stand out.

❗ Beware of work shuffling around inside a spacious box. Use packing material to ensure that the portfolio doesn't fall apart in transit.

Attention to detail

⭐ The level of finish is very important; designers note your attention to detail in the way a box is labeled and opened. More so than other disciplines covered elsewhere in this book, packaging designers notice how you have labeled your portfolio, whether it is easy to use, and whether it is neat. They are on the alert for a high-quality finish, whereas for other jobs, for example advertising, concepts are a bigger priority.

Interest in sustainable issues

⭐ Packaging design involves integrating the process with the product. In this project the die-cut title page makes use of the material itself without extraneous techniques. The form and the function are one, a desirable trait for packaging.

⭐ Using an elastic band as a binding technique is fun and simple.

⭐ This recycled-paper cover instantly transmits an understated approach.

ALSO SHOW: Sketchbooks

⭐ Before you are hired you will probably be asked to show sketchbooks. These should provide evidence of your methodology and show the standard of your work-in-progress. Interviewers will look for ideas, tear sheets, and ephemera. Become accustomed to keeping your sketchbooks neat and dense with ideas.

Celebrating the nondigital

⭐ The beauty of packaging is in the sensual and the textural, unlike mere 2D work. Therefore it is best not to produce an entirely 2D portfolio. Go nondigital and enjoy the fact that your portfolio is a physical experience aimed at designers who appreciate spatial design.

REALM OF
PINESS

a matter of chance"
Pride & Prejudice

Portfolio by Romchat Sangkavatana

Do ⭐

- Remember packaging is dependent on using sustainable techniques and on reducing waste and costs for clients. Always include a project that demonstrates how you are up-to-date with sustainable issues.

- Look for simple techniques. Although ambitious solutions to projects may be championed at college for thinking outside the box, they can look uninformed in professional contexts.

- Show that you actually enjoy making things. Too many students think that design is primarily an on-screen activity, and interviewers find this is simply not enough for a packaging studio. Demonstrate that you like materials, paper, textures, and print processes.

Don't ⓧ

- Don't forget to maintain your work. Monitor your portfolio and don't let ends get dog-eared or torn; a scruffy or dirty portfolio is a definite reason for rejection.

- Don't use only 2D for spatial work—computer-aided design is not everything in packaging design. Instead, show off ideas and use 3D where possible, and photograph ideas in context.

- Don't bring a lot of 3D. Consider the merits of shooting your work beforehand; short animation, shot in context, may show off packaging better than bringing it in person. Consider your journey—are you going by car or by public transport?

- Don't make your portfolio too flat either! Packaging is a fun area, involving people using things. When photographing 3D work, look for human qualities. Think about hands, feet, people; use friends and family as models; photograph people at work for a practical, human touch.

- Don't forget sketchbooks. Packaging designers look for drawing style and methodology. An A4 book would sit nicely at the back of an A2 book or in a box under 3D pieces.

Building your portfolio

Although the arrangement of contents in the archive box on the previous page appears random, the 3D pieces that sit on the top will be looked at first. Once they are taken out, work is viewed in sequential order. The following pages show a beginning, middle, and end that would work well for interviews at packaging studios.

Start with specifics

Prove your interest in packaging from the outset by starting with packaging-oriented projects.

TOWARDS SUSTAINABLE PACKAGING　　　**CASE STUDIES**

Figure 16
"Pack Green"
The stamp certifies and raise awareness that the product have not used unnecessary packaging.

1 All about packaging

⭐ For a packaging interview, this book works well as a leading piece because its content is wholly based on packaging. Including analytical writing shows that you are dedicated to this specialty.

2 Less can be more

⭐ The apple shows how packaging can be simplified by the use of a stamp. A neat idea like this works well at the front of any portfolio.

3 Display other skills

⭐ This hand-bound book—the visual outcome of a contextual essay—displays a high level of finish plus intellectual content.

⭐ The book proves that the candidate can research, write, and use print.

⭐ Inside pages demonstrate basic layout skills, balancing the 3D pieces elsewhere in the book.

Leave it out

Don't take everything you have ever done. Research the place you will be visiting and think carefully about what to take.

Poor-quality photography

- ❶ Although this homemade product, packaged and sold in a yard sale, is a fun example of initiative, the photography was rushed and not fully considered.
- ❶ Omit this photo, as interviewers will be frustrated that they can't see the whole packaging.

Repeating yourself

- ❶ If you have already included a conceptual piece (such as the red book shown left), there is no need to include a second piece, as it is duplicating skills you have already covered.
- ❶ This iPod plinth (above) has some merit, but if it takes too long to explain verbally, then it could slow down an otherwise successful interview.

4 Show diversity

- ✪ In contrast to the sustainable book (1, left), this simple timepiece belongs to the luxury market. The strong underlying 3D design refers to a 26-hour day; it is not bogged down by decoration, but uses simple typography.
- ✪ This works well toward the front, as it is memorable and the interviewer can pick it up and try it on.
- ❶ Beware not to put anything valuable in your portfolio. If you do, then seal it so that the portfolio cannot be tampered with before reaching the designer. Some samples are fragile or unique. If you are not sure, then use a photograph with a note saying that you can bring in the actual piece if needed.

The "main course" of the portfolio

Here traditional projects should make up the bulk of the portfolio.

5 Show freelance work if you have it

- ✪ This job was done for a clothing store and involved the creation of a logo for an event at a shop in Bangkok. Developed from the shape of scoops of ice cream, it is fun and humorous.
- ✪ The advantage of doing work like this is that it is printed and realized, unlike some college projects. It is a good idea to include some freelance work in your portfolio. You should explain it in a caption and say whether you were working to someone else's visual directive.
- ❶ If, however, you don't like the outcome of your freelance work, then don't include it.
- ❶ The project would be best presented as a mounted, captioned photo, which would fit easily in the presentation box.

············>

6 Mock-ups

⭐ Do not include easily breakable items such as these glass bottles; instead, photograph them. Here the white background helps to communicate the integral idea of diffusion.

❗ The typographic element could be included on concept boards. Detail would round out this brief.

Competition brief

Use competition briefs to build your portfolio of packaging. Many design organizations set these regularly (in the United States look up AIGA and SPD; in the United Kingdom D&AD—global entries accepted—RSA, and YCN online).

Designing to a brief helps you finish your work to a high standard and prepares you for the competitive world of the pitch.

7 Industry awareness

⭐ This entry shows awareness of industry standards. It doesn't matter if your competition entries did not win prizes; include them anyway.

⭐ This is straight-down-the-line design—less conceptual than the previous showy pieces. The product is not glamorous but demonstrates that this student can design ordinary items. Packaging studios need junior people for bread-and-butter work to bring in money.

Finish with a bang

The end section needs to be memorable. In this instance, the student opted for bright colors and humor.

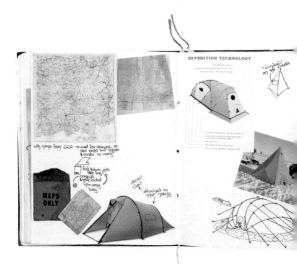

8 Vibrant finale

⭐ The end of a portfolio is often the place to put more personal work, like these bright posters for student societies.

9 Drawings

⭐ For a career in packaging, it is essential that you be able to draw. These sketchbooks display evidence of this, along with the ability to think through a process. If you don't want to drop off your sketchbooks, you could feature them on your website (see page 51), although you should make sure that any viewer can see the detail.

10 The last laugh

⭐ Don't let the portfolio trail off; instead, find an unusual uplifting end, like this 3D piece of an umbrella made from newspapers. Something fun and slightly irreverent means ending on a high. The student with his umbrella is confident and witty; look for something similar in your portfolio, re-photographing an item if necessary.

Digital portfolio: Packaging design

The following example examines a 3D portfolio remade for the Web. A digital portfolio can incorporate aspects of packaging design that a physical portfolio cannot, such as a product conveyed in video form, or a brand shown as a moving identity.

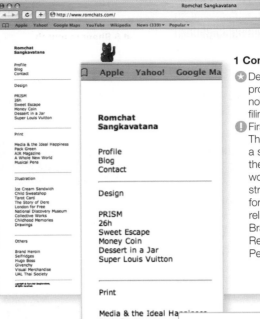
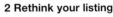

1 Consider your audience

⭐ Design your site for prospective employers, not just for your own filing purposes.

❗ First impressions count. The home page here features a standard menu list down the left-hand side. The page would be better with a stronger visual impression; for example, it could be relisted as Packaging, Branding, Competition briefs, Research, Sketchbooks, Personal projects.

2 Rethink your listing

⭐ For packaging and branding jobs remember you are branding yourself. Break down your listing to the main areas in which you are seeking employment. Keep it well organized so that it is easy to navigate, using a hierarchy of font sizes to guide the viewer to the sections you want them to see first.

3 Check blog content

⭐ A home page can be linked to a blog containing comments from other people about your work.

❗ Beware that blogs can be too informal and other viewers can add inappropriate material. Check your blog regularly and remove any content that you would not like an employer to see.

4 Link to other work

⭐ Link your site to other places where your work may be seen, perhaps a college website. This will also show the context of your education and identifies you with a peer group.

⭐ If you are self-taught, then link to any of the portfolio network sites that may feature your work (see pages 110–113). Your choice of peer group will say something about where you see yourself.

▼ 5 Include interactive work

⭐ Packaging designers need interactive skills, too, and of course you can't display those in your physical portfolio. Keep interactive work to the point and choose projects with a packaging bias.

❗ This musical piece has merit but lacks impact; unless it is explained well, it should be left out.

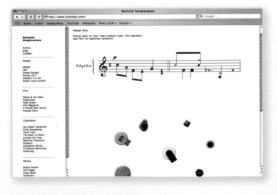

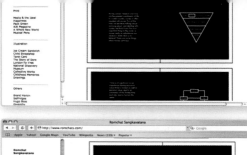

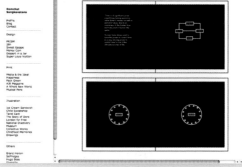

◀ 6 Share research

★ A great deal of research goes into packaging projects, and your website is a good place to show mood boards and development. Packaging designers like to see your thought process, but in an interview they may be short on time. Instead you can refer them to your website, which they can view in their own time.

★ The 26-hour watch (see page 47) emerged from thorough research that didn't fit well in the archive box, yet here it provides evidence to show there was substantial thought behind it.

7 Make the most of color

★ Bright and colorful pieces can really stand out from a plain Web background.

★ These images show the personality of the student, and affirm that he likes to get involved in the community—suitable qualities for a packaging studio, where you need to interact with artworkers, suppliers, and so on.

◀ 8 Feature sketchbooks

★ For packaging design work it is essential to show off your drawing skills. Sketchbooks on the Web work brilliantly, adding texture if you photograph them with a slight shadow (as shown here).

★ This student has recorded the pages that display his drawing skills, but you could also include pages of mood boards, collections of tear sheets, etc.

▶ 9 Show competition briefs

★ Packaging competitions are an ideal opportunity to show off your skills. If your entry is short-listed, link to the competition's main site; if not, link to the brief.

★ In your physical portfolio you would show the end product only, but in your digital portfolio you also have the opportunity to show the development behind it.

▲ 10 Include freelance packaging work

★ Even if you worked as part of a team on a job, you can still add freelance work. Explain your role and gain permission from the client.

★ In this case the ice cream sandwich was designed for a clothing range promotion. It is all the student's own work and is labeled as such.

❗ You may infringe copyright if you use a company's work, so it is always best to err on the side of caution—if you are not sure, leave it out.

Portfolio: Brand design

- **KEY SKILLS**
- **FIRST IMPRESSIONS**
- **BUILDING YOUR PORTFOLIO**
- **DIGITAL PORTFOLIO**

Brand design agencies look for designers who enjoy working with ideas in a real business context. Successful delivery of ideas is crucial, as is adaptability. Brand design, also called corporate identity design, is about using graphic skills to define business services, environments, and products. Designers are deeply engaged in the branding process, not merely with the surface output.

What do brand agencies do?

Brand agencies create new brands and refresh or reposition existing brands. All forms of communication are included in "branding." Brand management defines the core values of a client and the "brand promise." Brand development creates new products and investigates new territories.

Brand agencies create the brand's visual identity from their knowledge of the client—who their customers are and how they are reached. Agencies deliver the brand by designing all required elements, such as print, packaging, Web strategy, and interactive solutions.

Pros and cons

⭐ Branding is a fascinating environment related to economics, demographics, and marketing. To increase your knowledge, read or scan the financial pages of your newspaper or the business section of your news service.

⭐ Be a global thinker; work extends as far as the Web reaches. Employers look for "worldly" candidates—those who appreciate different cultures and embrace the global community.

❗ Brand design is not about surface design or pretty logos, but involves a ruthless energy for business and a love of commercial activity.

❗ It is difficult to get started and competition is fierce. Internships and placements are often unpaid.

Key skills a brand design agency looks for

Staying power

⭐ This airline project starts with a logo and then diversifies—the student has designed livery plus airport lounge interiors. Branding is not just a stamped logo but an identity with core values. Identity includes copywriting, application, color, and corporate gifts.

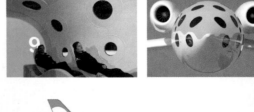

Understanding branding processes

⭐ Think big, then think at micro-level. These sample style sheets pinpoint which font and Pantone colors to use once another designer starts to apply the brand. Attention to detail means control of the brand.

⭐ Layouts look organized and use scale effectively, showing a flair for composition.

⭐ These images are striking enough to convince a potential employer that this designer could be trusted with a junior position, or at least a work placement.

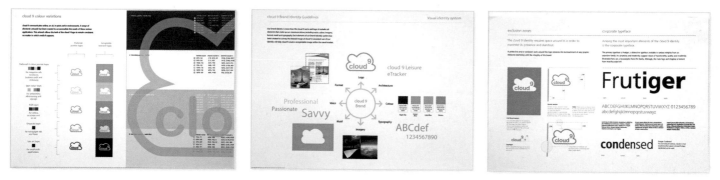

Drawing and visualization with software

⭐ This spread for a live competition on shop windows shows logo application, neatness, drawing, and research skills. A professional software program enables a carefully crafted visualization of a finished idea.

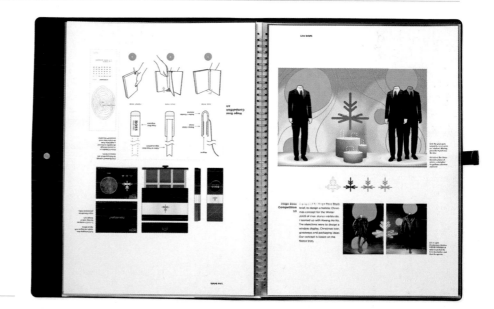

Ideas into digital platforms

⭐ Many brand agencies use interactive media. You don't need to be the world's best interactive designer; you do need at least a basic knowledge of programs. Show a fundamental knowledge—in both your résumé and your portfolio. It may not be evidence from a screen grab, but this photo of an interactive device is very convincing.

First impressions

You may like the sound of brand design if you are interested in information or the business and retail sectors. Branding is a broad arena; to guide you, the case study below examines the merits of organizing a wide-ranging portfolio.

See also →

Planning your portfolio See page 12

Size and shape See page 18

Advertising See page 62

Decide on CDs

❶ CDs seem old-fashioned when you can easily store your work on the Internet and give interviewers the link. However, there is no harm in leaving a disc behind, with your contact details, in case interviewers want to give the disc to others to see later.

Offer variety

⭐ The immediate impression given here is of a standard A3 portfolio, supplemented with a book, a CD, and a poster. The impact is of a student who has more than one type of output and enjoys different formats. Variety is essential; branding is less about designing corporate identities or logotypes, more about understanding different creative processes.

AMERICAN HAND LETTERING

ANDERS GODAL

Different formats

⭐ Include a poster to transcend A3 restrictions. Here the work is striking, and worthy of this size (see page 57).
⭐ If you are presenting in person, gauge the situation and know whether to unroll this poster first or at a later point; if you are not presenting in person, put the poster in a protective tube.

Books or non-A3 items

⭐ On the left-hand side of the portfolio, tuck in work that doesn't sit well inside plastic sleeves.

Take a bold lead

⭐ Use strong examples of brand design on the first page of your portfolio. State your intentions to be a brand designer loud and clear!

⭐ Find a sheet in your portfolio that looks dramatic, in this case a visual identity for a Norwegian festival. This sheet has a bold design using color and shape to exude confidence.

❗ Research the company and substitute the leading page if you feel it is unsuitable. The big mistake is to get so used to your portfolio that you fail to see it through the eyes of each new agency you encounter.

Follow up with a strong body of work

⭐ Include between six and ten projects, some of which should be extensive enough to explain how a campaign works. If you have more than ten, include the surplus in your digital portfolio and direct interviewers to the site by leaving a card with your link.

❗ Put a couple of strong branding projects at the front for an immediate impression; don't leave them at the back as a finale. More than other fields, brand designers are aware of how you present yourself. Be mindful of your personal graphic identity.

Do ⭐

- Be ambitious. As a junior you have little power; aim to become part of a team that can influence clients to take a more creative approach. The potential is huge. Hard work and ambition will keep you going through a potentially dull job as a junior.

- Include mood boards and idea development books. Branding is a lengthy process—you must show an interest in process as much as finished product. Make sure every sketchbook has a purpose and don't include your doodle collection.

- Include small freelance jobs if possible, clearly marked as done outside college to show initiative in gaining further experience. If you are switching to branding from another field, small freelance jobs will help to define where you want to be, and again demonstrate motivation.

- Find out industry-standard software requirements. Learn requirements at home using online tutorials.

Don't ✕

- Don't be self-centered. If your work is based on your personal take on the world, you may find branding unsuitable—it is undeniably about the client, not about you.

- Don't have a portfolio of one type of work, for example, playing with type or creating logos; branding is a broad field. Prove that you understand the rationale behind your items, the "why" behind the "what." If you don't know why, then you will fail when trying to explain.

- Don't let spelling mistakes slip through the net, particularly in copywriting. Check your work, then double-check it. If you are doing a course in American or British English but this is a second language, triple-check your text with a native speaker.

- Don't plan your work in chronological order, as you may have done in college.

rsfestivalen / The Bachelors Festival, branding - school project

Portfolio by Anders Godal

Building your portfolio

Consider how to direct the interviewer. This case study starts with examples in the plastic sleeves as core items, and leaves supplementary objects to be brought out as relevant.

Make a bold start

Be quick off the mark to impress as much as possible with your first projects.

1 Graphic identity

⭐ This project shows the full applied graphic identity for a Norwegian festival (for bachelors). Many parts are drawn together to form a visual campaign: drawings of a landscape, typographic logo, and a visual joke of dice.

⭐ The second page shows a simple application and the colors used to extend identity to items of underwear.

⭐ This is an effective visual identity to start, nothing too conceptual but reassuring to the interviewer.

2 Teamwork: global awards

1ST

⭐ This is an excellent project—it doesn't get much better than winning a top student award in a branding category. Include your entry even if you are not a prizewinner, as the interviewer will probably be familiar with this type of brief.

⭐ The brief was to create a brand for a radically new customer reward scheme. This solution extends to the full typographic visual identity for the interface design and includes the strong, simple design of shiny black packaging.

⭐ Next the student team submitted the advertising and mocked up a hoarding, providing the judges with both a poster design and a photo of that design in situ.

❗ Always credit teammates; think how you would feel if they did not credit you! For this reason, do not lead with this piece, which would imply that you had full ownership.

3 Further campaigns

★ Here is a more challenging and conceptual piece, showing experimentation with a typeface made with cress. Branding interviewers look for innovative thought as well as slick portfolios.

★ The challenging message is softened by the colorful and humorous visual delivery, showing evidence of art direction.

★ This piece works well up front and provides another vehicle for range of output, now using photography and vivid color in contrast to the technical and monochrome packaging of the previous piece.

❗ This would not be the best leading piece, as it is a classic "What if you had no boundaries?" kind of brief, so is not applicable to real-life campaigns.

4 More type and images

★ A few more ideas-based pieces fit in well here. Simple and graphic designs are useful to prove you can handle ideas perhaps at speed in a work environment.

★ This logo for a heavy-metal band is straightforward but elegant. Work like this indicates you can produce one-off logos.

··········>

Continue with a range of skills

After a strong start it's time to show a range of work to prove your worth even farther.

5 **Technical skills**

⭐ The folded-out poster and book give the interviewer an insight into the candidate's low-tech skills.

⭐ This hand-bound book, made in a bookbinding workshop, demonstrates skills such as hand–eye control and an ability to work outside of a digital format.

⭐ In a face-to-face interview a piece like this is memorable because interviewers can touch it.

"I MYSELF **HAVE HAD A** LITTLE ROMANTICISM FOR THE HEY-DAYS OF MY YOUTH *lately*"

AMERICAN HAND LETTERING
AMERICAN MEDIAL

6 **Is too much type too much?**

⭐ If you are trying to get at least a placement, you may be a candidate for layout and typographic tasks. Your ideas may win approval, but delivering basic layouts will always provide a way in.

❗ If you have too much work in your portfolio and are confident that you have shown off your layout skills, consider leaving straightforward layouts out of your final edit.

7 **Backbone of typographic skills**

⭐ Another typographic piece reinforces a taste for graphic color in type.

⭐ Typographic skills are useful for combining a big-picture idea with intricate detailing.

BOOK OF COMMON PRAYER

HIDDEN TREASURES
CENTRAL SAINT MARTINS
COLLEGE OF ART & DESIGN
Museum & Contemporary Collection

HIDDEN TREASURES
MARTINS
& DESIGN

THIS IS MY RIFLE THERE ARE MANY LIKE IT BUT THIS ONE IS MINE MY RIFLE IS MY BEST FRIEND IT IS MY LIFE I MUST MASTER IT AS I MUST MASTER MY LIFE WITHOUT ME MY RIFLE IS USELESS WITHOUT MY RIFLE I AM USELESS I MUST FIRE MY RIFLE TRUE I MUST SHOOT STRAIGHTER THAN MY ENEMY WHO IS TRYING TO KILL ME I MUST SHOOT HIM BEFORE HE SHOOTS ME I WILL BEFORE GOD I SWEAR THIS CREED MY RIFLE AND MYSELF ARE DEFENDERS OF MY COUNTRY WE ARE THE MASTERS OF OUR ENEMY WE ARE THE SAVIORS OF MY LIFE SO BE IT UNTIL THERE IS NO ENEMY BUT PEACE

8 Favorite campaigns

⭐ This freelance job of a drawn jungle-inspired logo shows the idea of plants connected to type. Interviewers can see that the student can both draw by hand and use digital programs to deliver images.

Finish with studio-oriented skills

To reinforce your suitability, remind the employer of how useful you could be in their studio.

10 Paid freelance jobs

⭐ Toward the end of your portfolio include examples of paid freelance jobs.

⭐ Again, remember to credit your contribution. Here the designer produced these illustrations for a Scandinavian health magazine. He did not contribute to the design of the magazine, so these images are best shown as tear sheets or marked with Post-it notes.

9 Student archive

⭐ Brand designers are busy people. Carefully select pieces to create maximum impact in limited time.

⭐ This foundation work shows an early interest in branding. Scale of production—in this case, branding on a school bus—is impressive and fun. If you have too much work, consider putting this in your digital portfolio.

❗ Some elements of this old college project may start to look dated. If you have a piece like this, decide if it is now worth inclusion.

11 Staying power

⭐ Take mood boards or something like this sketchbook. This example shows the process skills behind point 5 (opposite), and the link between the drawn letters and the finished book.

❗ Don't drag out a heap of sketchbooks with random ideas; show sketchbooks that relate directly to a piece, to illustrate how your ideas and research have contributed to the finished product.

Digital portfolio: Brand design

In turning a branding portfolio into a digital one, the challenge is first how to present your own identity. Some designers create pieces digitally without printing them out, so a physical portfolio is becoming less important, though it is not yet obsolete. The previous portfolio is examined below in digital format to see what works.

1 Brand your home page

⭐ The student's initials form a logo—Ag—that is memorable and graphic, and stamps his identity onto the page.

⭐ The slightly sarcastic line "This is where I will add…" shows individuality and a bit of fun with the format.

⭐ Work categories—Interactive, Personal, Print Identity, Print Illustration, Print Type—aid navigation.

⭐ The rotating orange sticker proclaiming "Available for hire!" adds an ironic tone. In an eye-catching package and an unusual menu, by asking to be hired the student has asserted both his character and his willingness to work.

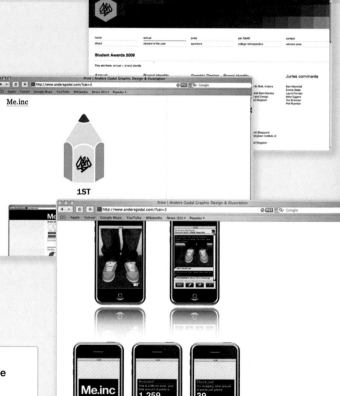

2 Lead with a colorful image

⭐ Vibrant colors look great on-screen. This poster for a club night in Oslo, created with a friend as credited, is fine as a portfolio frontage; however, with poster format users have to scroll down for full effect.

⭐ The poster does not appear in the physical portfolio—exclusion does not matter with skillfully executed pieces.

3 Competition award

⭐ As well as the competition feature, this section has room for descriptions of the brief and results, a link to the competition site, and includes judges' comments and public reaction. Judges' remarks reinforce interviewers' opinions, as these competitions are industry benchmarks.

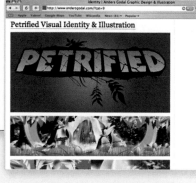

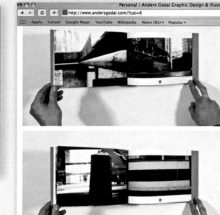

4 Crisp and graphic logos

⭐ The North Sea logo benefits from landscape format. The site layout allows a strong explanatory caption for each logo.

⭐ The Petrified logo shows vibrant application of color.

5 Use striking images

⭐ These on-screen images, combine photography with illustration. They add color to the website and are evidence of a real freelance job.

6 Suited to digital

⭐ Digital portfolios can display types of work not seen in the physical portfolio.

7 Campaign details

⭐ Use the Web to emphasize details such as this cress letter. Experimentation with scale through the occasional large-scale item helps to maintain visual interest.

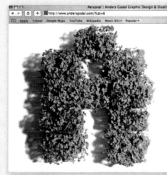

8 Extra illustrated work

⭐ Drawing is not universally considered a branding requisite, yet an ability to draw fluidly on-screen is a valuable skill. It is believed that accomplished designers need essential drawing skills—observation, storytelling, and hand–eye coordination.

9 Final words on personal work

❗ Quirky designs are found lurking on most student websites. Apart from the speech bubble, there is no clue to the purpose of this collaged logo, and it may look misplaced. Consider putting such images on your blog instead.

⭐ This is correctly filed under the category Personal and Illustration. Clearly mark up and caption such images as personal.

Portfolio: Advertising

- **KEY SKILLS**
- **FIRST IMPRESSIONS**
- **BUILDING YOUR PORTFOLIO**
- **DIGITAL PORTFOLIO**

The backbone of this portfolio is ideas, ideas, and ideas—the presentation of which must demonstrate both problem-solving skills and staying power. Show that you can step into your customers' shoes and that you are a strategic thinker. Boundaries between the roles of strategists, creatives, and copywriters are often blurred.

Key skills for an advertising agency

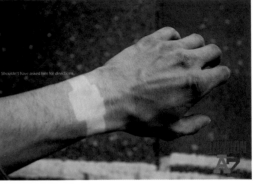

Immediacy of ideas

⭐ Use bright ideas with instant impact. Visual puns and strong ideas show a creative brain. Here an everyday item is used with a twist, creating an immediate and memorable impression. An accompanying notebook displays the original sketch on the bottom left page.

High-impact content

⭐ This self-initiated campaign for an interiors and lifestyle magazine shows creative copywriting, using the tagline "Antidote to the Urban Environment." It is straight to the point and cleverly uses the environment itself to provide the backdrop to the campaign.

*Wallpaper**

*ANTIDOTE TO THE URBAN ENVIRONMENT

⭐ In another example of use of copywriting, this competition entry was a finalist in a global design competition and plays with the existing branding of a furniture store.

KNOWYOUCANREPLACEIT

Wallpaper*

Designing for campaigns

⭐ Advertising should demonstrate alternative ways of seeing the world, like this budget bus-travel campaign, which points out the true value of a bus fare (dinner with Mom and drinks with Dad).

⭐ Simple ideas and clear messages can be very effective. Here, creative thinking rather than a range of skills should be demonstrated. For more inspiration and samples, see the Global Students Awards Annuals.

What do advertising agencies do?

Advertising agencies provide communication between clients and customers using clever ideas and campaigns. They produce words and visuals for print, TV, Web, and radio, and digital advertising such as viral marketing.

Traditional larger companies have both creative and planning departments. In the creative department of a medium-sized agency, hierarchy varies, depending on country and agency.

Companies need young creatives primarily to generate ideas and to communicate or invent content. Trainee teams may be hired for internships.

This business is attractive for young people with an affinity for brands and youth culture, yet undoubtedly hard to break into without some kind of work experience.

Staying power

⭐ Include work to demonstrate the development of an initial clever idea. One-off ideas are not enough; show that you can stay with a concept, through different outputs and areas of the brand.

⭐ Here a slogan is not enough; context matters more. Putting the sticker on the bike seat delivers the message, connecting the user with the focal point. Photographing work even in such a simple way can be very effective.

Pros and cons

⭐ This is a fast-paced and exciting environment using up-to-date technology. Ideal candidates have in-depth knowledge of current affairs, business, and trends.

⭐ You will have an active interest in both high culture (art, literature, music) and low culture (street fashion, trends).

⭐ This is a great option if you work best with words, in teams, under pressure, and think independently.

❗ Initially you will work hard and maybe long hours. Graduates may have to work unpaid because of fierce competition for jobs.

❗ You will be pushed to come up with ideas even when your best ones are rejected. Don't consider advertising if you crumple under pressure.

❗ How ethical are you? Advertising is commercial; you may work on accounts that you don't believe in.

First impressions

Keep your work in a simple format, like this A3 portfolio with fixed sleeves. A fancy archive box may not withstand the rigors of quick interviews or portfolio reviews. You might drop your book off for a senior creative, so it must tell a story without you there to explain it.

See also →

Planning your portfolio
See page 12
Size and shape See page 18
Brand design See page 52

Take ideas books

⭐ True advertising creatives never stop having ideas and are on the go 24/7. The two young women behind this portfolio work together and keep constant notes of ideas they have every day. This little treasure book contains the best of those ideas and shows both keenness and total dedication to a life in advertising.

❗ As a student, you must be prepared to allow your ideas to be seen by everyone (see panel on page 69).

Take sketchbooks

⭐ At the beginning of your career you can include sketchbooks to strengthen the imagery in your work. Take more than research, as this alone is not sufficiently engaging in interview situations; include ideas in development for a brief.

❗ Don't take sketchbooks filled with random doodles and drawings.

❗ As you become a more mature creative, perhaps a few years after college, you will have enough work in your portfolio and won't need to take such sketchbooks.

Choose robust books

⭐ This A5 board-bound sketchbook is strong enough to survive many interviews.

Label your work

⭐ This little ideas book contains content that is different from the bulk of the portfolio, so remember to use clear labels on sketchbooks like these to tell the viewer exactly what they are looking at.

Interactivity in person

⭐ You may want to take your laptop. It is easier to open up and to show and explain your work personally, than it is for an interviewer to find a computer in the office to check your website. Make sure all your files load easily to save time.

❗ Never, ever drop off your laptop inside your portfolio.

Let the work tell the story

⭐ The first page—a campaign brief—is a finished poster; as a completed piece of work, mounted with a clear border, it aims to sell more pens. This strong idea of an obsessive writer is instantly communicated.

❗ Tell the story from start to finish; otherwise selected pieces will fail as effective advertising messages.

Cohesive elements

⭐ This designed header is a neat device that runs throughout the portfolio, describing succinctly each featured piece. It is particularly useful when there are numerous parts to a campaign.

Portfolio by Danielle Emery and Natalie Turton

Do ⭐

- Go to agencies for advice on your portfolio or book. Ask for a book review. If you don't know anyone at an agency, read the advertising press. Keep an eye on news about award winners. Phone agencies you like and ask for creatives' names, numbers, and e-mail addresses, then call them or e-mail your work to them.

- Write down interviewers' comments so that they know you are listening and taking their advice seriously. You may well see them again—it is useful to show them new work and tell them you made changes and improvements according to what they said. Interviewers will be flattered that you liked their suggestions.

- Send a small thank-you after a portfolio review. If interviewers liked a campaign, send something as a reminder with a thank-you note. Always thank people. It's free, it means a lot, and not everyone does it.

Don't ✕

- Don't have outdated views—the days of the copywriter generating words for the art director are long gone. Now creatives both write copy and design ads without inclination to one skill or the other. Some top creatives work on strategic planning and present their ideas to clients.

- Don't give up. Keep e-mailing and calling—be persistent even if you get no reply. Advertising people are busy; they are not being rude. Take an original approach.

- Don't rely on one person's advice because you will receive contrasting opinions of your work from the various people you see. Instead, wait until you have seen ten people, then tally up which campaigns were liked best and remove the least popular ones.

- Don't feel you have to go it alone; find a partner and be part of a creative team. Build a portfolio and start gathering advice and feedback. Ask people to recommend other agencies you could see.

Building your advertising portfolio

Plan for instant impact—agencies thrive on clear communication above all. Include campaigns even if they are mock-ups. This case study of a team of two successful graduates shows why advertising portfolios are different from others in this book.

Start with your strongest idea

Your portfolio must make an immediate impression; you will be judged on the quality of ideas within the first few pages.

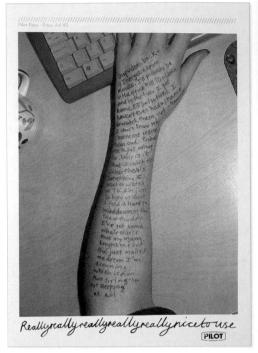

1 Show your copywriting skills

⭐ This poster campaign checks all the boxes for a positive start. The brief was to promote a simple item: an everyday pen. Writing on different surfaces is a playful and direct idea, accentuated by the scrawled tagline ("Really really…nice to use"). Every feature underlines that the team can create ideas, write copy, and visualize outcomes.

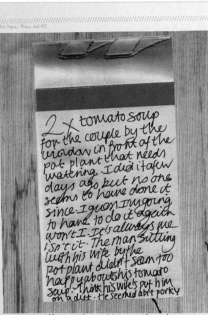

2 Illustration of product use

⭐ This delivery card left by the mailman provides a further example of product use (the pen being so nice the user couldn't stop writing) and extends the campaign.

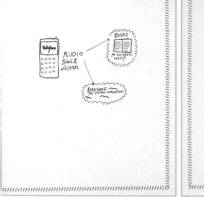

Call Vodafone to block certain numbers for a night.
Eg. ex on valentines day.

If you turn your phone off at night there's a special number your closest friends can call to turn your phone on again if they desperately need to get in touch.

ahh help!!!

3 Dare to be different

⭐ An unusual feature is this recurrence of ideas for a phone company, at intervals throughout the portfolio, like commercial breaks in a TV program. None of these pieces is fully realized, but each contains another idea.

⭐ These concepts show an understanding both of the fundamentals of medium and of how the brain retains then displays information. Try an interspersed campaign like this only if you are very confident.

If i can put this in your bag, what could i have taken out?

ENDSLEIGH
INSURANCE

Continue with further campaigns

In the middle of your portfolio, broaden evidence of your ability to constantly generate new ideas.

4 Service not product

⭐ Clients often require abstract solutions; if they offer services, not physical products, you can't use pack shots. For this insurance brief, viral marketing uses an original idea of fake wallets, dropped into people's bags by a team of helpers, with the tagline "If I can put this in your bag, what could I have taken out?"

5 Ambient campaign

⭐ Vary pace and tone with ambient media. Here a travel campaign stimulates imagination and engagement: It transforms urban landscapes as canvases to transport you elsewhere. The Sistine Chapel's ceiling is painted on a London Underground platform, and Venice's Bridge of Sighs is reproduced on a canal bridge. These mock-ups convey ambient concepts very clearly— ideas matter more than image quality.

·········➤

6 Humor in cliché

⭐ Using thought bubbles, this campaign for an MP3 player mixes humor with graphic cliché to emphasize customer autonomy—you can't predict what a listener is actually choosing to hear.

⭐ The mock-ups are made from photos the creatives have taken themselves or found on the Web, then altered using collage.

7 Interactivity in print

⭐ This retail campaign for a bookstore assumes customers are so thoroughly engrossed in reading that they neglect to notice their environment. The campaign suggests a solution: a wipe-clean book cover that tells other passengers the subway stop at which the reader needs to disembark.

⭐ The concept is extended to provide customers with a map for the lost-and-found office and taxi numbers for when they miss their stop.

8 Label internship work

⭐ A label here states "work done on placement." Differentiate speculative work done for academic assignments from that created in a professional context. Clearly state which agency you did the work with.

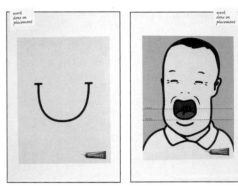

9 Art-direct your work

⭐ In this amusing campaign "Let them think you're gay," the team arranged their own photo shoot to capture the exact image they wanted, instead of using stock images.

⭐ Knowledge of styling helps to strengthen visualization. Draw on any general design background to re-create the image you have in your head.

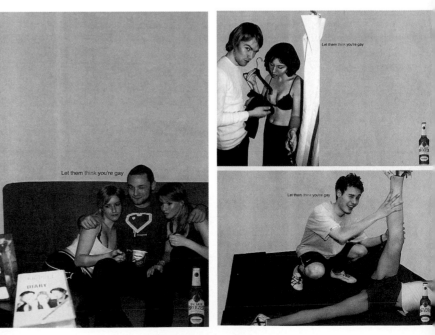

Finish with ideas development

Ending on a carefully selected creative note will leave the right impression.

10 Creative thinking

⭐ Creative thinking can be a constructive way to round off an interview. If interviewers want to see more and the meeting has gone well, show drawings to reinforce skills. This sketchbook underlines content creation, showing copy lines and planned thoughts.

⭐ Subject diversity is pulled together by felt-tip. These pages illustrate a bold sense of mark making; no 2H pencil hesitation; instead, brightly colored letters emphasize strong statements throughout.

11 Strategic planning

⭐ Use of lists and plans of action shows that this team can think and plan strategically, an essential skill for advertising.

12 Be an encyclopedia of ideas

⭐ These students have decided that their ideas books are worth presenting, and have heavily edited their thoughts down to the strongest few. Ideas are therefore both memorable and digestible. Interviewers do not have to dig through a thick sketchbook; selection is done for them.

Will they steal your ideas?

Have you come up with an amazing idea that could be worth something? If you are afraid to show this in case it is "stolen," you need to learn more about the advertising industry.

First, we all have access to the same cultural influences, so ideas connected to these common experiences can occur at the same time in different places.

Second, yes, your idea may trigger a thought in another mind, and creatives may act upon that trigger. However, as a graduate there is not much you can do about this. In return for their precious time, creatives expect to see exciting new work and ideally will enjoy looking at your portfolio.

Develop the ability to always come up with another amazing idea—if one gets away, regrettably, you'll need to shrug, move on, and create an even better one. You are in the business of generating new concepts; each should be better than the last.

Digital portfolio: Advertising

Why put your portfolio online if the aim is face-to-face interviews? The answer is twofold: First, you can show moving images; and second, you may have to send digital work first just to get a foot in the door for an interview. See Chapter 3 for advice on digital platforms.

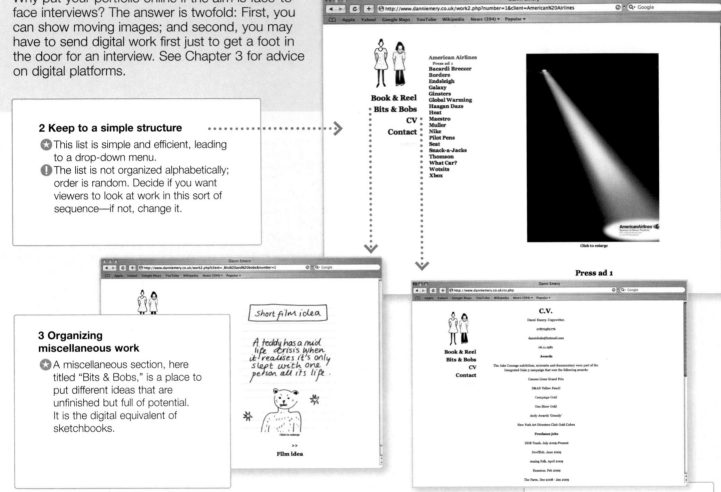

1 Sell yourself without selling out
⭐ Make your home page personable and not too arrogant. This simple drawing of the two students makes them seem accessible and approachable.

2 Keep to a simple structure
⭐ This list is simple and efficient, leading to a drop-down menu.
❗ The list is not organized alphabetically; order is random. Decide if you want viewers to look at work in this sort of sequence—if not, change it.

3 Organizing miscellaneous work
⭐ A miscellaneous section, here titled "Bits & Bobs," is a place to put different ideas that are unfinished but full of potential. It is the digital equivalent of sketchbooks.

4 Information from résumé
⭐ This résumé clarifies internship experience and links campaigns to agencies. The student is not taking credit for any of this work; instead, she is very clearly referencing context. (See pages 120–122 for more information on résumés.)

Best practice tips

⭐ If you work for some of the most reputable agencies, your website will start to fill with high-quality content. Make sure that your résumé details which agencies you worked for and when. Within the advertising community, showing work is acceptable as long as you explain your contribution. If in doubt, leave it out.

⭐ As a student, you may have worked on a team, as here, but on graduation have changed partners for various reasons. Again, be sure to credit partners, old and new; be generous on your website or blog and link to their sites. Always behave professionally—you never know when you will need each other again.

❗ Take care when putting clients' work on your site. Be aware that brands don't like to be misrepresented—keep any private experiments off the Web.

❗ The ad business is a small world and you may get caught out, so be cautious.

5 Increase content

⭐ Include content that appeals more directly in moving format—this campaign extends to video.

6 Break up the digital look

⭐ This bright, cartoon-like sketch benefits from on-screen display—the bold felt-tip lines and colored letters really stand out, and provide a welcome change to the sleekness of the digital platform.

7 Show physical pieces again

❗ Screen size means you can't see this poster in A3 size, and writing detail is lost here.

⭐ Back up the on-screen image with the physical item, as examined on page 66, to show full impact from essential elements.

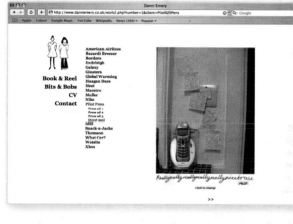

8 Use Web tools to your advantage

⭐ This car-magazine campaign uses a visual joke. The image can be enlarged on-screen for full impact—there are no fussy techniques. The idea works instantly on the Web as you flick through more pages quickly; at a click, another image appears, giving a very satisfying experience.

Portfolio: Book design

- **KEY SKILLS**
- **FIRST IMPRESSIONS**
- **BUILDING YOUR PORTFOLIO**
- **DIGITAL PORTFOLIO**

In the perfect portfolio for book design, typography should form the foundation. Page layouts are essential, so prove that you can work with text and image on a page. This portfolio should be pleasing to the eye and a joy to touch and experience; books are held and appraised, so reinforce the connection between hand and eye.

Key skills for a book designer

Passion for type

⭐ Show your love of typography in all shapes and forms. Examples of book arts reflect your ability to sustain interest in type. Here the student has combined a contemporary cell-phone spelling for text with calligraphy.

Creative covers

⭐ A variety of covers (right) is eye-catching and shows your commitment to book design. This series was designed for a competition, set by a publishing company, for college students.

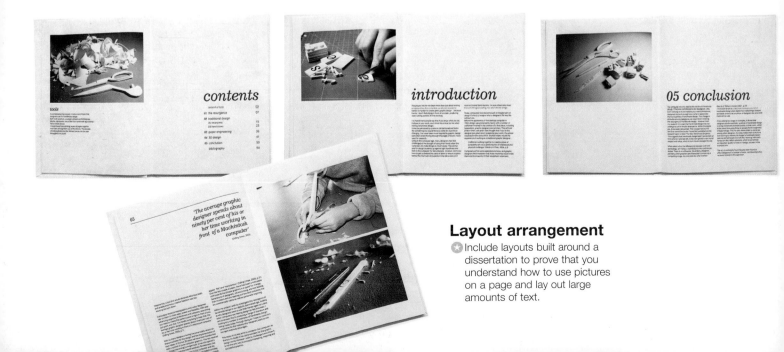

Layout arrangement

⭐ Include layouts built around a dissertation to prove that you understand how to use pictures on a page and lay out large amounts of text.

What do book designers do?

Book designers design printed material in paperbacks and hardbacks, in fiction and nonfiction, and work on book proposals for both publishing houses and independents. You may secure a junior position in a big publishing company as an intern, or be hired as a freelancer to collaborate on a project. You should try to meet people at industry events such as conferences and lectures.

Juniors should try to start wherever they can and learn on the job. Most book design companies look for someone who can absorb industry jargon and practices, and who takes on board feedback and constructive criticism.

Illustrated books

⭐ Book design involves storytelling through many pages, using cropped images and layout. This designer is driven by his talent in illustration, organizing story around visuals, and demonstrating that he could be trained on the job.

Respect for the reader

⭐ Book design should be both functional and aesthetically pleasing. Consider using a well-known text—as the in the piece above—to show your visual and textual skills. The pictures here are vibrant and bring the story to life; the text is left simple and is easy to read.

Storytelling

⭐ Coming up with images for book covers can be a real challenge. This desktop wallpaper shows a talent for selecting images with impact that set the scene, transferable skills for book cover design.

Pros and cons

⭐ Pace of work changes when deadlines approach, and you must work quickly and accurately.

⭐ Book crafts and old-fashioned arts like letterpress and font design are alive and well. Like-minded communities meet to discuss these crafts and uphold good practice in a digital age.

⭐ Online communities offer advice to those starting out—look up type clubs, book design forums, and online educational sources.

❗ Unless you have the right software knowledge, expect long hours and low pay initially, because of the labor-intensive nature of building templates and pages. You must be proficient in book design programs and may have to teach yourself.

❗ If you have a general design portfolio, then you may need to build up book design pieces. Either set yourself specific projects or go to a class to get some ideas.

❗ You will need a knowledge of print production, some of which can be learned only on the job with correct technology that is hard to match at home, for example, technology to send pages straight to plate.

The Grapes of Wrath
Original Paintings

KITSUNE NOIR

First impressions

It is immediately clear here that this student likes the printed word and enjoys making books. The body of work printed on A3 sheets looks promising, but the small items at the top give the portfolio unique and intriguing qualities. Engage with the interviewer: Starting with booklets helps break the ice to initiate conversation—interviewers will pick up the books and appreciate the craft skills involved.

See also ➞

Planning your portfolio See page 12

Size and shape See page 18

Magazine design See page 90

Invite interaction

⭐ This untitled book project is bound with a paper band. Color is stark and eye-catching, yet, once opened, the book offers depth of typographic detail. An engaging combination of attractive binding with professional delivery is a strong start.

Carrying the box

⭐ The slim archive box is neat and a compact A3 size. It is carried in a simple canvas bag; in a drop-off situation you could switch to a more robust portfolio case.

⭐ Both carriers protect the work and can hold any extras like a résumé or booklets.

❗ Don't take too much. Book design is a specific profession; concentrate on the task in hand. Do show your ideas, but don't show every piece you did at college. This substantial body of work benefits from compact presentation—an ideal balance for an interview at a busy publishing house.

❗ The loose books may slide around. Consider how to pack items carefully if you must drop a portfolio off; never mail a box like this without taking utmost care (see page 14 for packing tips). Keep one or two copies of hand-bound books in pristine condition at home.

Show a bound example

⭐ This book is bound with a rubber band. Once released, black covers fold out to a poster, just under A2 size. Though the work has been photographed and reappears later, try to include it at the front as well. It is difficult to show solely with a photograph that this poster folds out—it is more effective in real life.

Oh, so you're an artist?

If somebody asked you what you did, you couldn't say graphic designer because then you'd have to explain that and you'd bore yourself right out of your skull. You had to say "Well I'm a commercial artist" and that would put an end to it.

Ivan Chermayeff

Focus on samples

⭐ These book covers show that this work belongs to a potential book designer. When building your portfolio, choose a first page that illustrates your ambition for a publishing career, even if you have no experience in this area.

Include color and texture

⭐ Book designers don't always think in black and white; a splash of color makes a portfolio a treat. Interviewers look for something original. This brown-paper stitched booklet is finished with a red rubber band—simple materials reflect stylish austerity. Before interviewers even know what the book entails, signals suggest a carefully designed piece with consideration for materials.

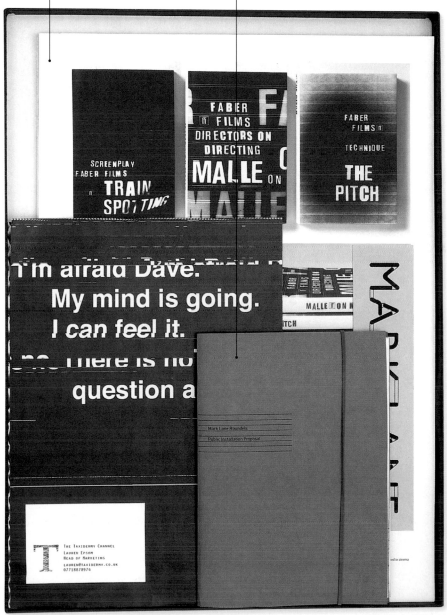

Portfolio by Ed Cornish

Do ⭐

- Demonstrate your passion for books and reading; show that you have chosen this field because you like to read. Include work that transcends a brief or that goes into greater detail than usual.

- Include any evidence of letterpress or book crafts skills as additional features. Photograph handmade booklets if you don't want to take them. Many designers create small book projects; some attend bookbinding evening classes for basic techniques. These optional additions help make your portfolio more interesting, and more tactile than flat printouts.

- Keep any nonbook work at the back or online to illustrate broad skills.

- Include a résumé with your portfolio and specify your software skills. Ascertain the standard software requirements for the publishing industry and learn them at home using online tutorials.

Don't ⊗

- Don't include irrelevant college projects. Instead, focus on core book design skills that interviewers want to see, for example, using the correct font size in body copy, text flowing in columns, and typographical hierarchy. Keep extraneous projects to a minimum.

- Don't print layouts smaller or larger than they should be; actual size shows that you understand that on-screen text size does not correspond with printout text size. Many designers who don't print out mistakenly use large body text, which then looks too large on the page.

- Don't forget to check for spelling errors, and keep your portfolio neat. Attention to detail is a primary attribute of book designers.

Building your portfolio

Aim to impress with ideas and content; emphasize equally confidence in typography and layout skills. As a student looking for an internship, ensure college work is both impressive and distinctive. If you are self-taught, or switching from another discipline, show fundamental layout skills and a willingness to learn on the job. This undergraduate portfolio shows the basics needed to build a convincing portfolio for a junior book designer position.

Start with combined text and image skills

Small booklets that can be picked up with pages to turn will appeal to the book industry.

1 Contrasting elements

⭐ Use simple materials with confidence. Choose bright colors to offset natural colors, as found in this brown kraft paper. The bright invitation livens up this otherwise monochromatic piece.

⭐ Inside, a strong graphic identity for a public installation is invented around an abandoned subway station. The layout is dynamic and uses a neon-inspired typeface to evoke an urban feel. A confident use of text sizes enhances the A5 page, indicating knowledge of the full potential of design across double-page spreads.

2 Grid skills

⭐ Text layout is open using a floating column grid to leave white space, revealing a basic knowledge of grids. A portfolio like this should display a variety of grids, so make sure you do not simply reuse the same one.

3 Information in covers

⭐ The last page shows skillful use of space across the inside back cover. The designer has considered the full potential of the booklet's card cover and added a flap to the fore-edge to maximize information.

4 Information in centerpieces

⭐ Another fold reveals a centerfold and another type of information graphics, an illustrated map. Use different parts of a book to add breadth to content.

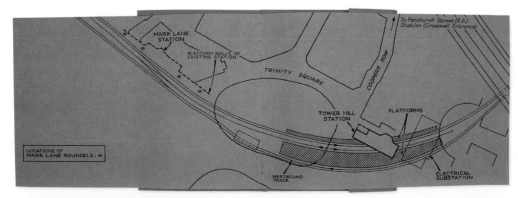

5 Emphasize the principal subject

⭐ The gatefold of this book reveals three A6 booklets, all related to the subject of a contextual project: altermodernism.

6 Text, hierarchy, and image

⭐ Body text is broken up by use of bold hierarchy, and pictures illustrate themes. Use complementary elements to create interest and cohesion.

❗ Combining text and image effectively is not as easy as you may think. The skill of using pictures over pages to tell a story is of value. These three sections help the narrative.

7 Scope in artwork

⭐ Pages from the middle booklet show designed copy and exploration in artwork. Unlike magazine design, book designers usually work with given images—they may not have the power to art-direct an image to fit the text.

⭐ A very basic grid can incorporate different types of images.

Continue with A3 card sheets

Densely laid out A3 sheets create a compact portfolio; this looks more accomplished than a thick A2 volume of work.

8 Experimentation in typography

⭐ These book covers show keen interest in type forms and experimentation. The caption reflects this: "My entry to D&AD student award brief for typography; to design a series of covers for Faber and Faber's books on film. I took inspiration from the Perspex lettering used in cinema signage, and made photograms for the covers."

⭐ Instead of a found font, create letterforms to reinforce the subject matter. Here the use of black and white is cinematic and confident. It fits the context, as the photograms are directly connected with the subject matter of light and dark.

❗ Add color; don't veer toward a monochromatic portfolio—the overall effect can be dull. Look over your portfolio once it is finished and maximize any color you have used.

•••••••••>

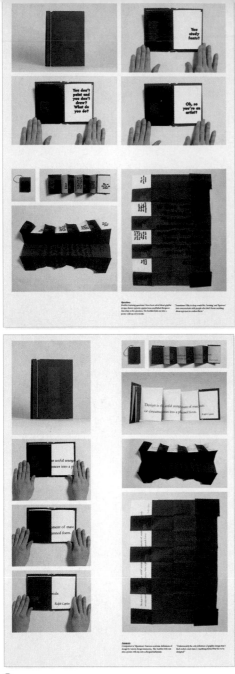

9 Caption if needed

⭐ A caption, titled "Questions," explains the background to this photographed black booklet: "Booklet featuring questions I have been asked about graphic design, shown opposite quotes from established designers that relate to the question. The booklet folds out into a poster." This A3 sheet clarifies precisely what the booklet is about. The caption is succinct and informative.

⭐ A caption, titled "Answers," explains the accompanying booklet in a companion A3 sheet: "Companion to 'Questions' features academic definitions of design by various design luminaries. The booklet folds out into a poster with my own colloquial definition."

10 Continue with an experimental piece

⭐ Next comes a bit of color and an unusual format. Involvement in a student interim exhibition shows motivation to work beyond the minimum and to get involved with college social life. Graphic identity transforms a diagonal element into a parallelogram-shaped perforated ticket. Posters were pinned up and tickets ripped off, thereby reusing the poster itself.

⭐ Identity is extended both to a VIP invitation and to name tags clipped on display boards. Overall presentation is clear with informative captions. The explanation demonstrates an eye for detail and an ability to tell the story of the work. This poster was done by a team of four students, and credit is clearly given.

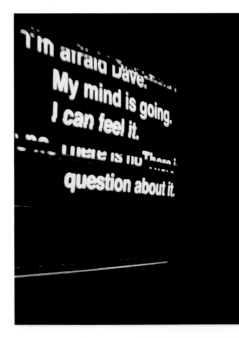

11 Show interest in type as image

⭐ This caption for a typographic movie poster illustrates a willingness to experiment: "Quote from '2001—Space Odyssey,' as said by HAL the lethal computer as it is being turned off by an astronaut it has already tried to kill. The type has been digitally corrupted, inspired by Hal's malfunctions in the film, then was photographed on a television screen." The poster shows an ability to find content within letterforms that can tell a story in themselves. In a competitive marketplace where students often use the same favorite fonts, it is refreshing to see original work like this.

12 Include extra projects?

⭐ These shots for an animated TV ident illustrate an interest in art direction and photographic style.

❗ These shots could be omitted once new work comes in, as there are other strong images in the portfolio.

13 Include a competition entry

⭐ This concept subverts a standard warning arrow and bends it over to create another. A successful shortlisted entry to a design competition set by London's Design Museum, although not book design, shows interviewers that the student is willing and able to extend skills beyond the course syllabus.

14 Visual play

⭐ Here the student and his friend re-create Photoshop effects in real life: from the top, the Paint bucket tool, Erase giant eraser, and Gussain Blur shot in a photo studio.

⭐ A clever visual joke could provide a humorous moment in a nerve-wracking interview. Here it also serves to demonstrate knowledge and experience of setting up a simple photo shoot.

15 Letterheads

⭐ Most of you will have a letterhead; whether to include it varies with each interview. If you have had positive responses to your work and the idea is strong, keep it in. If other work better demonstrates creative and layout design skills, leave out the letterhead or put it on your digital site. This letterhead is an extension of the TV ident above (12). The design adds texture in the capital T—arguably a reason for inclusion.

End with core interests

As a sign-off, bring attention back to your core skill and interest in book design.

16 Back to books

⭐ This exhibition catalog is a video artist's work shown as a loop. The book is an accordion-fold format from a composite strip that loops around and is a continuous narrative, having neither beginning nor end. A succinct finale combines an interest in graphic design with a flair for exploring and challenging book design practices.

Digital portfolio: Book design

Consider how best to show off typographic layouts. Some choose a basic PDF, others a website with links. Video content features less in book design portfolios than in advertising, for instance.

1 Strong start, wide selection

⭐ A strong home page, the name big and bold, makes an immediate impact.

⭐ Viewers can choose what they want to see. Without a hierarchy, selection options can resemble a box of chocolates, where viewers have control. This home page has concise captions to describe pieces effectively, indicating innovative work through simple use of words and images.

4 Connect work

⭐ This internship work was featured on the employer's blog, providing great coverage for the intern and a huge confidence boost. Features from external sites are about connecting with like-minded people. The community of practice around typographic interests is growing online.

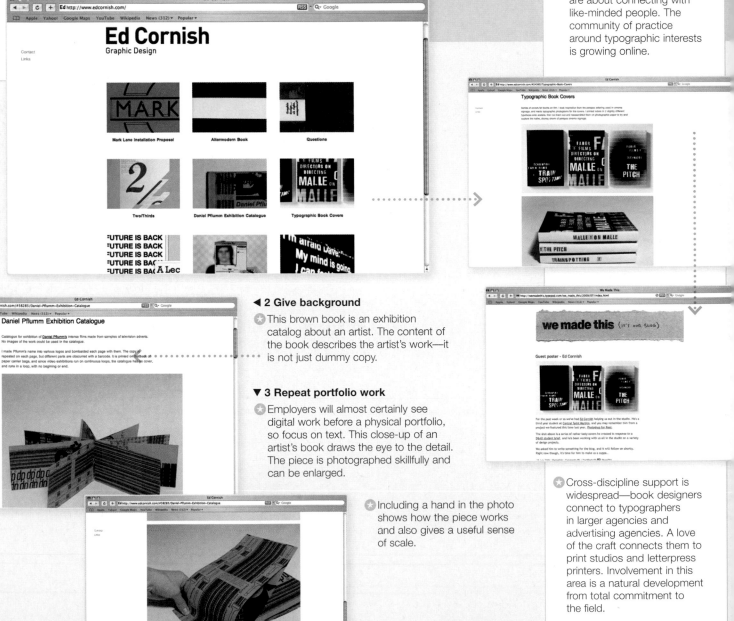

◄ 2 Give background

⭐ This brown book is an exhibition catalog about an artist. The content of the book describes the artist's work—it is not just dummy copy.

▼ 3 Repeat portfolio work

⭐ Employers will almost certainly see digital work before a physical portfolio, so focus on text. This close-up of an artist's book draws the eye to the detail. The piece is photographed skillfully and can be enlarged.

⭐ Including a hand in the photo shows how the piece works and also gives a useful sense of scale.

⭐ Cross-discipline support is widespread—book designers connect to typographers in larger agencies and advertising agencies. A love of the craft connects them to print studios and letterpress printers. Involvement in this area is a natural development from total commitment to the field.

▲ 5 Support your peers

⭐ This joint project is covered on a friend's blog and linked to the designer's site. Support each other for maximum coverage and to find work. A lifelong commitment to design begins with the friend from college and continues after graduation. This student already has well-established contacts.

⭐ This Photoshop joke has major impact on the site—a funny graphic design piece for all to enjoy.

6 Show typographic work

⭐ These plain posters have powerful impact on-screen. A simple typographic display can be surprisingly effective.

◀ 7 Include digital concepts

⭐ Show you can think digitally by including examples of your interactive work. In the digital portfolio, this design for a screen saver can be demonstrated fully. A screen shot of the monitor reveals how the typographic screen saver works in the studio environment.

8 Show variety

⭐ This signage project introduces landscapes and figures to the site, maintaining a varied context. The photo breaks up the heavily typographic content and helps mix things up, which keeps viewers interested.

Portfolio: Magazine design

- KEY SKILLS
- FIRST IMPRESSIONS
- BUILDING YOUR PORTFOLIO
- DIGITAL PORTFOLIO

Magazine design is a specific skill. It is visual journalism, telling a story with words and pictures. The editor communicates a certain editorial message, and designers create the visual identity, adding life and flair. Fashion and lifestyle titles exude this skill, using images and typography to entertain and inspire.

Key skills a magazine design company looks for

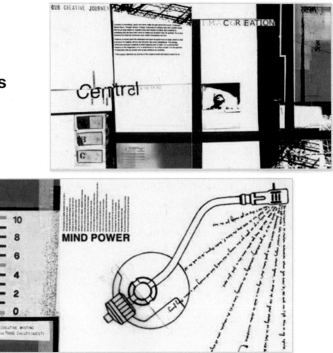

Passion for magazines

⭐ Many magazine designers are passionate about this medium above all others and see themselves as directors of content too, which leads to self-publishing. This student project became a publishing venture and shows awareness of the complete package, from idea, to images, and even to story editing.

Knowledge of publishing

⭐ This project, on newspaper design, shows research and layout skills. The student is interested in newspaper design and shows elegant use of headings, subheadings, a five-column grid, and captioning.

⭐ This analytic presentation, more intriguing than the standard A4 format, demonstrates understanding of skills in context.

Art direction and planning

⭐ These pages emphasize art-direction skills—photos are styled and shot with a vision for the finished story. Instead of finding pictures online, the student photographed his friend, directed into interesting shapes, in simple yet stylish layout. The images have rawness and energy.

⭐ Considerations of lighting again indicate that this designer took photos while thinking ahead about how the images would appear on the page.

What do magazine designers do?

Art/design directors create visual identity; design teams follow this vision and create pages in the house style. Junior designers work for art directors and help turn images into page layouts, paying attention to detail while maintaining the design vision.

Consumer magazine publishers produce titles in-house. Each magazine has an art director and a small team of designers who work on two or three titles plus marketing materials. In business-to-business publishing, designers work on five to twenty titles. Designers are also employed in contract publishing agencies, where magazines are produced for big brands and corporate clients. Independent studios design magazines for various publishing clients, now often online, as some titles exist solely as PDFs.

Samples of layout

⭐ Include simple layout examples, even if made up. If resources are limited, find content around you. This student photographed his typography studio at college and invented a story for experimentation.

⭐ Dummy copy doesn't matter in student portfolios, but headlines and introduction should be real text, without spelling mistakes.

Pros and cons

⭐ Magazines are team environments, connecting people with overlapping interests. This communal practice usually creates a pleasant environment and excellent networking opportunities.

⭐ Despite the threat of online publishing, printed glossy magazines are still popular. There are valued skills of printing and color reproduction to learn, and producing printed work can lead to greater job satisfaction.

❗ If you are unhappy in teams or with critical advice from senior art directors, consider another option.

❗ You need to love typography and setting columns of text. The reader is all-important, the designer mostly anonymous.

❗ With self-publishing abounding, it is mistakenly thought that anyone can design magazines and skills are undervalued. You must work hard to prove that skills are valuable and can make a huge difference to the success or failure of a title.

First impressions

Magazine designers look for examples of student pieces and preferably of work experience. You will probably find that an A3 or A2 portfolio will form the base of your work—add other magazines or print projects such as zines or sketchbooks. Include strong examples of typographic skills, plus evidence that you can sequence pictures as stories across spreads, showing narrative skills.

See also →

Planning your portfolio
See page 12
Size and shape See page 18
Book design See page 72

Tags and captioning
⭐ The green sticky notes assert that only the tagged pages were designed by the student. If he were to include the whole magazine, there would be confusion about exactly what he had worked on. Notes clarify input without the interviewer having to ask.

Standard portfolio with added items
⭐ This portfolio uses a straightforward approach with ring-bound pages in portfolio sleeves, an accomplished traditional format. Keeping the format simple enables the interviewer to see the quality of page design. Putting these magazine tear sheets at the front suggests that there is a lot to look at. You can tuck them in at the back, but then the impression is more monotonous. Using your work experience first may initiate a conversation and be a positive starting point in an interview.

Small items in a large portfolio
❗ Small detailed books need to be picked up and handled, and do not sit comfortably within large glossy sleeves. Consider adding a slim archive box or a museum box if you can find one.
⭐ It is worth keeping these items in for a welcome change of scale so that not all of the work is A2 or A3.

Printed spread

⭐ Seeing your design on work experience in print is exciting and impressive—show it off. This gives the interviewer confidence that you can see through the entire process, from layout through proof stage, to sending to print.

⭐ Even though this work was completed under the direction of a senior designer for an independent publisher, it still proves capacity for teamwork.

Statement on the right-hand page

⭐ The first page of a portfolio makes a statement about your priorities so consider what is best for you. The vertical format means you can't start with a series of magazine spreads. In this case the student does not yet have a strong magazine cover, so instead leads with a graphic poster about the Albertus typeface to show interest in typography.

Do ⭐

- Go with a work placement under your belt—take tear sheets to show pages. Be honest about what you did under direction; interviewers understand that you have worked to a house style.

- Give credit to art directors to demonstrate you can take direction. Include this information in your digital portfolio too.

- Take heart that many top designers are self-taught or came from an illustration or arts production background. Take a short magazine course or typography class to build your confidence, and your portfolio.

- Learn any relevant software—use free Web tutorials and practice at home if you can. If you get a placement and are unsure of a software task, don't be afraid to ask for help, but also realize there won't be time to teach you everything on the job.

- Join editorial networks such as SND in the United States and Europe, and EDO in Britain. Freelancers need to stay in touch with designers, so go to lectures, exhibitions, and events (look online for details). If you do not live in an urban center, join blog communities (search online or in magazines for details).

Don't ⊗

- Don't forget to rearrange your work, whether for a financial publisher or for a funky design collective. Prepare beforehand by researching company publications.

- Don't have a narrow portfolio of one type of work as this is a broad field, requiring interests in typography, layout, image making, branding, and Web design.

- Don't have spelling mistakes, particularly if your work involves headlines and introductory text. Check your work with built-in spell-checkers and, assuming you don't trust the results, use a dictionary to double-check.

Building your portfolio

Though you may start with a general graphic design portfolio, you should prioritize layout and art direction instead of problem-solving briefs or 3D packaging projects. This portfolio has pieces selected, in sequence, for a magazine design company.

Start with a solid typographic foundation

Whether you are self-taught or have taken type classes in college, prioritize typography.

2 Type and images

⭐ Following the typographic start, this zine project experiments with type and images, using magazine format for personal style development. Use mock-ups as visual frameworks for future releases.

1 Typographic exploration

⭐ Showing that you know your Albertus from your Arial matters. Many modern fonts were designed for on-screen use only, to be avoided in fine print; some traditional fonts work less successfully on-screen, as fine serifs were designed to hold ink. Typographic pieces indicate a solid background knowledge of type.

Continue with relative skills

After an experimental start, aim to slow or regulate the pace.

5 More type and images

⭐ Use of a three-column grid exhibits proficiency in standard book design layout and thinking outside format. A piece like this convinces interviewers that if hired, you can deliver simple layouts within the confines of a grid set by someone else.

··········➤

3 Captions with your photos

⭐ The designer shot some photos to create the right look; friends supplied other shots as a last resort. In the zine the student has used fashion caption format to identify his photos.

⭐ A common problem is how to credit what you or other contributors did. Be clear without overstating the point. Use credits both on the work and for photos within captions. In the magazine business particularly, image creators and writers are credited, so follow this professional practice.

⭐ Integrated captions and blanket statements reinforce messages.

4 Play with format

⭐ The student experiments with spine and trim size. Have some fun and play—although not always ideal in large-scale runs, in short runs this lovely folded zine within a magazine is achievable. Interviewers value new layouts and formats.

·········➤

Fractures from Anxiety, short stories
by Marcus Bastel

Anxiety is a physiological state characterized by cognitive, somatic, emotional, and behavioral components (Seligman, Walker, 2001). These components combine to create the feelings that we typically recognize as fear, apprehension, or worry. Anxiety is often accompanied by physical sensations such as heart palpitations, nausea, chest pain, shortness of breath, stomach aches, or headache.

Marcus Bastel was born in Frankfurt in 1967. He was internationally educated in fine art practice, studying for his degree in the UK before pursuing post-graduate studies in Amsterdam. He has won several awards and his video work has been shown across Europe. Screenings in the late 1990s in Amsterdam, Glasgow, Manchester, Milan and Paris were accompanied by invitations to publish. Early writings include art catalogues and his first collection of short stories Part of the narrative first published in 2004. Having taken some time to focus on his career development within the Computer room of the BAGD course at Central Saint Martins College of Art & Design, Bastel is now creatively a force to be reckoned with. This long awaited second volume draws together still more of the different strands of his writing to date. He lives in London with two cats.

ISBN 978-0-713-99973-3

a Penguin book

Fractures from Anxiety

Marcus Bastel

6 Book covers

⭐ This student project (left) for Penguin Books reemphasizes skills in set format. The designer has created and set the illustration within the confines of a paperback cover and includes a conventional back cover. Magazines and books are closely related; don't limit your portfolio necessarily to only magazine design.

⭐ Book covers can be used in your portfolio to break up editorial content. These colorful competition entries (above) are designed to work as a series so that the spines create maximum impact when stacked together.

RDCL/VD

22.05.09 — 22.06.09

AVANT-GARDE ARCHITECTURE RETROSPECTIVE

7 Academic text

⭐ Identity for an avant-garde architecture exhibition is designed as a pamphlet. More abstract than a commercial magazine, images show the student can research a subject, organize main points, and present work in a legible, intelligent way. Use of a two-column grid with floating captions is simple and convincing.

8 Identity from image-making skills

⭐ This identity for an audiovisual collective includes packaging and print design, and features a perfect abstract image. Such pieces reinforce a range of skills and visual thinking.

1S Superstudio was an architecture firm, founded in 1966 in Florence, Italy by Adolfo Natalini and Cristiano Toraldo di Francia. Superstudio was one of major part of the Radical architecture movement of the late 1960s. The founders had gone to school at the University of Florence with Archizoom founder Andrea Branzi and first showed their work in the Superarchitettura show in 1966.

In 1967, Natalini established three categories of future research: "architecture of the monument"; the "architecture of the image"; and "tecnomorphic architecture". Soon, Superstudio would be known for its conceptual architecture works, most notably the 1969 Continuous Monument: An Architectural Model for Total Urbanization.

Many of their projects were originally published in the magazine Casabella.

Natalini wrote in 1971 "...if design is merely an inducement to consume, then we must reject design; if architecture is merely the codifying of bourgeois model of ownership and society, then we must reject architecture; if architecture and town planning is merely the formalization of present unjust social divisions, then we must reject town planning and its cities...until all design activities are aimed towards meeting primary needs. Until then, design must disappear. We can live without architecture..."

Superstudio was influential on architects such as Zaha Hadid, Rem Koolhaas, Bernard Tschumi.

2S Founded in Florence by a group of radical young architects in 1966, Superstudio was at the heart of the architectural and design avant garde until its dissolution in the late 1970s. Through photocollages, films and exhibitions, it critiqued the modernist doctrines that had dominated 20th century design thinking.

"In the beginning we designed objects for production, designs to be burned into wood and steel, glass and brick or plastic - then we produced neutral and usable designs, then finally negative utopias, forewarning images of the horrors which architecture was laying in store for us with its scientific methods for the perpetuation of existing models." This was how

Superstudio described its work in a catalogue the group produced to accompany the 1973 exhibition Fragments From A Personal Museum.

Superstudio was then at the fulcrum of avant garde thinking in architecture and design. Ever since it first surfaced in 1966 at the Superarchitecture exhibition in the Italian town of Pistoia, Superstudio had been among the most vociferous of the radical design groups which were challenging the modernist orthodoxies that had dominated architecture for decades.

By questioning architecture's ability to change the world for the better and the boundless faith in technology expressed by earlier, more optimistic groups such as Archigram in the UK, Superstudio raised issues which have preoccupied successive generations of architects and designers from Studio Alchymia in late 1970s Italy and to the Memphis collective in the mid-1980s, to contemporary figures like Rem Koolhaas and Foreign Office Architects.

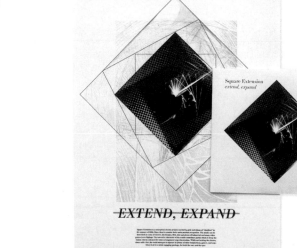

Square Extension
extend, expand

EXTEND, EXPAND

09·05·09

Finish with work experience

The end of your portfolio is the best place for work placement projects, to reinforce your employability.

9 More image making

⭐ These energetic illustrations, created on a work placement, understate typography, ensuring that the fashion brand is the principal message. Including these abstract images provides a visual break in the run of the portfolio.

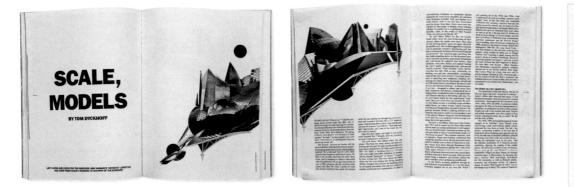

10 Talk about your placement projects

⭐ These spreads, created during a six-month placement, exhibit layout, typographic, image-making, and research know-how in a professional setting. The opening spread features dramatic typography following the house style set by senior designers.

⭐ Pages are dramatized by the illustration running across the fore-edge and to the next spread, pulling readers on. Again, design is plain, simple, not overcomplicated. Grab the opportunity to create pages and develop images around you for maximum impact.

11 The last word

⭐ Here is another illustration created by the student, this time full-page, illustrating a famous fashion writer's piece. Senior designers trusted this student with the work, which proves their faith in him. This piece would end an interview on a positive note with an endorsement of character.

Building a portfolio without going to college

Many self-taught designers can build a reasonably successful portfolio of book covers or magazine spreads without going to college. You can see briefs on the Internet (look on university websites or see *D.I.Y.: Design It Yourself* by Ellen Lupton) and take the initiative by designing pages yourself. In college or evening class you should receive valuable feedback and typographic direction. If you don't, ask for your money back!

However, college education is not always possible, in which case you will have to work harder for critical input. There are mentor programs and Internet forums where you can communicate with designers.

If you are self-taught, include portfolio work that shows initiative, solid typographic skills, and a natural flair for page design.

Digital portfolio: Magazine design

Although magazines are best viewed in physical form, digital portfolios are sent separately, to be viewed before and after interviews. In turning a physical portfolio into a digital one, you can fit in a large archive that is too big for a fifteen-minute interview. However, you can't view actual size or typographic detail well on-screen; instead, a sense of art direction and layout aptitude and style is emphasized.

1 Use your home page to full advantage

⭐ Many magazine designers use a simple PDF portfolio. PDFs enable you to tell your story in a straight line, from beginning to end; avoid anything complicated that may obscure content.

⭐ Don't worry if your portfolio is not interactive—you are being judged on site layout, not construction.

❗ The list menu on the left-hand side is underused. Although it clarifies titles for users, they do not know the names of pieces— great work lies hidden in the titles "Radical Void" and "Enhanced Performance." Design your site for other people once you start to look for work.

❗ Maintain your site as an outward-facing presentation, not a site for filing purposes.

Series of editorial illustrations for the magazine's 10th anniversary special issue. Completed during a six-month placement at TANKFORM.

◀ 2 Show off work experience with care

⭐ An immediate impression is that if you put a piece in your portfolio, you designed it! Be careful: Specify any contributions. Here the caption explains exactly what the student claims to have done.

❗ Once viewers scroll down to illustrations, all is revealed; however, viewers may not scroll down. Put the work you want them to see at the top.

❗ Placing the two photos side by side on-screen would be better for the viewer.

◀ 3 Work you no longer have

⭐ This example shows limited-edition prints. If you no longer have work in good enough condition to include it in your physical portfolio, you can still include it here.

⭐ The use of bright color looks great backlit on-screen, to brighten up the largely gray website. Composition skills will appeal to art directors.

◀ 4 Layouts repeated in the physical portfolio

⭐ This piece will be shown at interview, but a caption explains it in detail. Try to keep up-to-date with captioning as you add work—this helps viewers understand pieces in your absence.

Fashion and culture magazine blad. First issue provides a visual framework, i.e. typography, layout, style of photography, and illustration for future releases.

  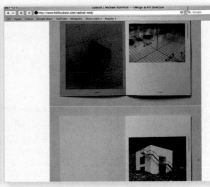

▲ 5 Extended projects

⭐ Include the full project in your digital portfolio and take a few pieces to the interview. If more detail is requested in the interview, you can turn to your digital portfolio.

❗ Do not use your website as a dumping ground. Make sure you are proud of all work on display.

⭐ Shoot layout work using powerful lighting, and check focus as you shoot. Magazine designers enlarge Web images for typographic detail, so keep it as crisp as possible.

❗ These layouts have gone a little gray and the photography could be improved. Magazine designers look for attention to this kind of presentation detail.

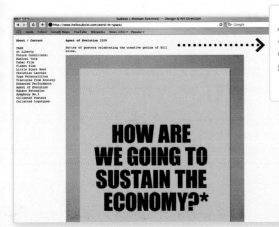

Agent of Evolution 2008. Series of posters celebrating the creative genius of Bill Hicks.

HOW ARE WE GOING TO SUSTAIN THE ECONOMY?*

"Economy that is FAKE anyway! What's going to happen to the arms industry? How are we going to continue building nuclear weapons if we all start experiencing unconditional love? You know what I mean?!" - Bill Hicks

▲ 6 Detailed Web shots with captions

⭐ The student has produced a series of typographic posters about comedian Bill Hicks. Visual messages can belie meaning: The bold design suggests a quote with gravitas, yet the caption reveals a visual joke, and the underlying meaning a comic response.

⭐ Telling typographic jokes is a useful skill in magazine design, as you are often using minimal wording to communicate ideas. Be careful going from language to language, however, as jokes do not always translate; use them carefully without causing offense.

❗ Swearing (not shown here) can make you look unprofessional. Minimize or delete swear words. Art directors prefer to see a wider vocabulary that eliminates the need for bad language.

▼ 7 And finally

⭐ Magazine publishers ask page layout designers to create logos for editorial sections and for marketing materials. Include an array of logos to convey versatility and knowledge of branding design.

Navigation no-no's

The content of this portfolio is impressive; however, navigation could be improved via the home page. Like a magazine with a weak cover, readers won't open it, and content is wasted if the cover fails to do its job. Apply this thinking to your home page: What will make viewers click on through?

Employers may not bother to click on obscure headings, but may simply give up. They could have looked at twenty portfolios before yours. Ask yourself: Will mine stand out?

Act soon—you never know when your portfolio will be called upon. Your work may be visually strong and full of impact, but if it is hidden behind a page that obscures content, you may not get that interview!

design
for online promotion

by Chris Jones

There has never been an easier, better, or more exciting time to put your work online. From whichever corner of the globe you are in, you can create and publish movies, magazines, comics, viral ads…the list goes on. Get it right and your work can reach millions of people, a perfect vehicle for an aspiring graphic designer.

This chapter examines the different types of online portfolio—websites, blogs, and networks—helping you decide which is the best option for you. The pros and cons of each are discussed, and helpful format comparisons, dos and don'ts, successful examples of each format, and detailed case studies are featured. Your branding is crucial in creating the best first impression on potential employers, so spend time thinking about this important point.

chapter

3

Equally paramount is the design and usability of your online portfolio, so this section also covers information delivery and encourages you to think about site navigation, ensuring that your online space is user-friendly and delivers the required information quickly and easily.

Portfolio: Online

- **FIRST IMPRESSIONS: HOME PAGE**
- **SITE NAVIGATION**
- **BUILDING YOUR ONLINE PORTFOLIO**

In the online age, a digital portfolio is an essential component of how you present yourself. If you don't have your work online and available 24/7 you can be certain you are missing out, but you need to make sure you get it right!

Future clients and prospective employers expect to visit a Web address and view your work online at their leisure. With this comes the opportunity to showcase sound, animation, film, and more, but it also means you are competing potentially within a global field. Online portfolios must work across a range of screen sizes, technologies, and connection speeds. An additional challenge is a widespread familiarity with format; creating impact online is especially difficult.

See also →

Portfolio: Website See page 102
Portfolio: Blog See page 106
Portfolio: Network See page 110

Pros and cons of digital portfolios

★ Viewports are mechanisms through which people can see your portfolio. The choice is vast and growing—perhaps you have an iPhone; ideally (and more likely), a conventional 12-, 15-, or 30-inch screen. These devices make your portfolio highly portable, opening up new and immediate employment opportunities.

★ With multimedia at your fingertips, you can take advantage of sound, animation, and movies to create a unique and memorable "experience."

★ Multiple portfolios, pitched at different audiences, help target specific users and provide content they are expecting to see.

★ Online viewing empowers viewers; they can browse in their own time and pick and choose what they delve further into.

★ You can reach an international audience in a global market.

❗ You need to make sure you have the right software and plug-ins for laptops and other viewports, to provide a reliable, problem-free viewing experience.

❗ Before promoting your online site, double-check that everything works, using a range of computers and Web browsers.

❗ Your portfolio website must be hosted on a server; your server must be up to speed to deliver high-quality images fast.

❗ Online portfolios still need well-written text, checked carefully for spelling and grammar. Online or off-line, a thoughtful and beautifully presented portfolio stands out from the crowd. Avoid making your text so small that it cannot be read.

❗ Unlike off-line presentation, online you do not have full control over how the pages are viewed.

❗ Never forget that you are one click away from being turned off and forgotten.

Format comparison

There are a number of different options available to those wanting to present work digitally. The following lists detail three main areas: a website, blog, and network. Each has benefits and pitfalls, and in some cases a combination might be the most suitable option. Choose the format that best fits your skill level and objective for putting your work online.

Website

⭐ Build your own site to learn extensive skills for online design and to show technical ability.

⭐ You have total control over every aspect of your website, assuming in-depth technical ability.

❗ You need to be proficient in a number of different software packages and have a good understanding of programming.

❗ It is very easy to build a website that looks amateurish—be aware of professionalism and image at every stage.

❗ This discipline requires a considerable amount of time.

Blog

⭐ Blogs are increasingly used by mainstream companies as major features of their online presence, and, as such, being able to build and update blogs is a core skill.

⭐ Use the many prebuilt templates that are available, enabling you to build better than you would otherwise find possible.

⭐ Blogs are easy to update.

⭐ Blogs do not have to look like traditional ones with lots of user comments. Many "websites" are in fact blogs.

❗ There is a potential lack of overall design control, unless you thoroughly understand the programming language, with a resultant loss of quality control.

Network

⭐ Networks are often free and require minimal technical knowledge to set up.

⭐ Benefit from the power of networks and reach many more people than you could otherwise do with your own website.

⭐ Networks are easy to update.

❗ Design, and therefore image, is usually restricted by the site.

❗ Sometimes use of your own domain name is prohibited.

❗ Some networks are shared by many users, so it can be difficult to make your work stand out from the rest.

Do ⭐

- Consider your chosen field and select pieces accordingly. If this is branding, for example, do not focus on photography, however strong your photography skills.

- Take care to categorize work into relevant sections.

- Keep your online portfolio up-to-date and maintain a schedule for uploading new work.

- Write short descriptions carefully; provide written context if needed—viewers may not always understand projects and work. In links to a website, for example, have you specified your responsibility for design or programming, or did you create the logo or copywriting? Clarify what you are showing and why.

Don't ✕

- Don't put all your work online; as iterated throughout this book, selection is key.

- Don't allow spelling and grammar mistakes to creep in.

- Don't assume users will spend time downloading large files; always try to have a version that works for speedy download or display without any need for additional plug-ins or software.

Technical skills

Presentation of digital work may seem daunting at first. Without digital skills, you would have a whole set of tools and terminology to learn. However, unless you want to specialize in digital design, it is not essential to become a Web wizard to get your portfolio online.

First impressions: Home page

Home pages are critically important: If users are not instantly captivated online, they may close the window, and you are history. This is your shop window; make people want to come inside.

1 Start by grabbing attention

⭐ Plan to update your home page, perhaps by replacing work weekly, or by programming random images, to keep visuals constantly new and stimulating.

2 Don't make them wait

❗ Your site must load without delay on average connections—don't assume everyone has super-high speeds. If your page hasn't loaded in a couple of seconds, chances are visitors have lost interest or patience and gone elsewhere.

3 Be user-friendly

⭐ Fill your home page with powerful content and images.

❗ Avoid pointless animation with "skip intro" or "click to enter" messages. Users don't like them; neither do search engines.

4 Clear signposting

❗ Make it easy for the user to navigate your site (see pages 98–99). Explore other sites and note which are easy to navigate and why.

❗ Ask friends, family, and colleagues to find their way around your site, and to report any obstacles and frustrations.

5 Use average screen size, and fill it!

❗ This page (below) underwhelms—not only is it lacking impact in visual appeal, but the page title (top of window) is left as "Untitled Document." Engage and impress; don't display lack of either interest or technical ability.

Name designed as logo.

Clearly categorized work under the headings Illustration, Web design, Graphic design, and Animation.

Thumbnails of work entice the viewer to click and reveal more.

Opportunity to click on and view designer's blog.

Testimonials and endorsements are included as a "Featured article"; the calendar shows the article is recent.

Comical and friendly illustrated characters convey personality and make the site memorable.

Informal contact form inviting the viewer to "Talk to me."

6 Provide an insight

⭐ This kevadamson.com page (above) promotes personality through every integrated element—users gain an immediate sense of Kevin Adamson's work and skills.

⭐ Search engines will like this site because it has a balanced ratio of text and image, and the text that is there is keyword rich (see page 116).

⭐ Name and tagline ("Video and film") clearly indicate site name and purpose.

⭐ An individual logo, though simple, adds to the uniqueness and memorability of this site and the designer's name.

⭐ The domain of duk-duk.com is represented by the logo, but the designer's name alongside it is also clear.

Name/Logo/Tagline

⭐ Another important decision is name presentation, whether a logo or more simply written. Generally this should be in the top left corner of your website so that users can immediately identify your ownership. Link logo to home page, a convention followed by most sites.

Choosing a domain name

At graduation shows, a common scenario is to pick up a thoughtfully designed and professional business card or postcard, only to have this impression destroyed by an e-mail address along the lines of "drunk-everyday@gmail.com." Whereas such an appellation may have seemed a witty idea at the time, it is not an encouraging representation for a prospective employer. Your domain name is the same. People will access your online portfolio via your domain name—choose it with care.

You may want to reference your specialty: petra-loves-type.com, or perhaps your name: stefangraphicdesign.com. Whatever you pick, make sure it's both available for registration and presents a professional image.

Avoid low impact

⚠ Search engines value front page content. Avoid single-page animation leading to an "enter" sign; instead, use inviting images and words to engage users; otherwise, visitors may leave before exploring the work inside.

Site navigation

The navigation of your site is essential to the entire user experience. There are many sites with alternative and clever navigation schemes, but generally you are better to keep things as obvious and as easy to find as possible. Devise a clear system to categorize your work.

► From anywhere within the Georges Moanack site (www. g-moanack.com) it is simple to navigate elsewhere. Five main sections identify principal areas, and subsections lead to individual projects.

Georges Moanack
Industrial Designer

+ HOME

+ PORTFOLIO

Ultra Lead

Hang

Blind +

Trazo (pedestrians)

Trazo (vehicular)

Greenwash

Miss Flect

Loop

Hinoki

Modul

Exo

+ ABOUT ME

+ NEWS

+ CONTACT

Be careful

❶ Avoid links to pages "coming soon"— delete the pages until they are finished. Look efficient and up-to-date.

❶ Don't be too clever. There are many sophisticated techniques, but simple and clear navigation is generally more user-friendly.

Showcase your work

Showcasing styles and methods is vital. Much depends on your technical skills and choice of platform. Given the know-how, you can do almost anything; without it, you will need to work with the options available from the blog or software you are using.

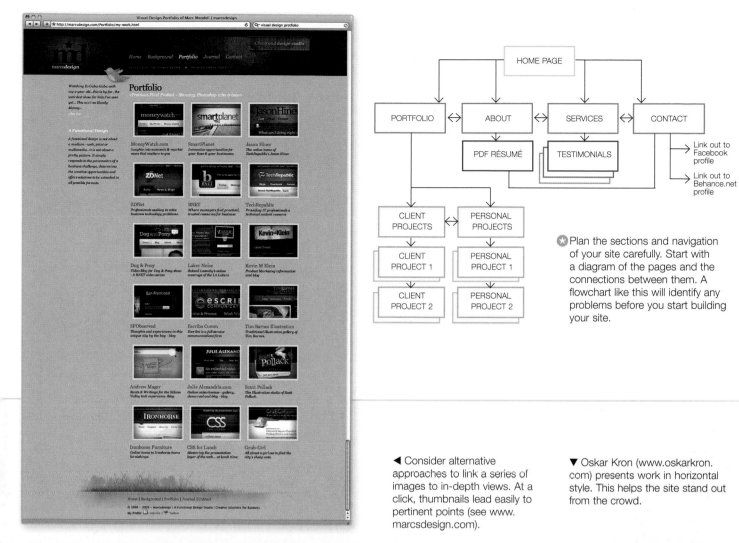

★ Plan the sections and navigation of your site carefully. Start with a diagram of the pages and the connections between them. A flowchart like this will identify any problems before you start building your site.

◄ Consider alternative approaches to link a series of images to in-depth views. At a click, thumbnails lead easily to pertinent points (see www.marcsdesign.com).

▼ Oskar Kron (www.oskarkron.com) presents work in horizontal style. This helps the site stand out from the crowd.

Building your online portfolio

Your approach to your online portfolio will depend upon your specialty, and you should review the Digital portfolio sections throughout this book. There are, however, some general considerations.

Always aim to clarify your skills for anyone who does not know you. Some designers specialize, others generalize—either way, get specific skills across. Don't pretend to be an expert at everything; very few designers are. Interviewers are acutely aware that statements such as "StefanGraphicDesign: fine artist/film editor/photographer/graphic designer/3D visualizer" are too good to be true.

Essential pages

No matter your specialty, these sections should be the core of your digital portfolio.

About you
• Keep this section short and to the point. Include a résumé, or link to a downloadable PDF.
• Try to inject a little personality into what you write.
• Avoid rambling—readers do not want to know what you had for breakfast.

Your contact details
• Make contacting you as easy as possible. Consider using an online form, such as the example bottom right (www.alexcohaniuc.com).
• Keep contact details up-to-date.
• Avoid unprofessional addresses (e.g., dave-the-slacker@gmail.com).
• Do not link to your Facebook profile if this contains any kind of content that could be regarded as unprofessional.

Your work
• Your portfolio should be well organized, by type of work or chronologically.
• Offer a selection of your best work.
• Flag any award-winning work or any piece that has had press coverage.
• Keep your work up-to-date and current.
• Avoid overloading your site with work.

Are you content-less?

⭐ The introductory screen for Hana Stevenson's site (www.hanastevenson.com) is a fun animation.

❗ However, at the time of print, clicking on many of the links reveals a frustrating "I'm not here right now, come back later" message. In the rush for an online presence, it is an all-too-frequent occurrence to quickly put together a website, then neglect to update it. This makes for a very frustrating user experience. If work is not ready, do not draw attention to it—better to omit the link and consider creating a one-page presence (see page 117).

❗ It looks more professional to have an e-mail address relating to your domain name than to a Gmail or Yahoo! account (e.g., info@domainname.com).

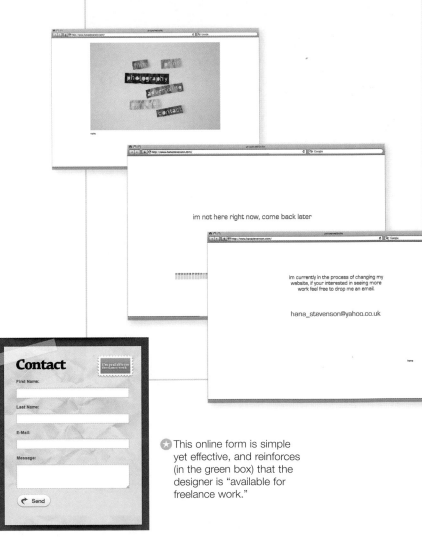

im not here right now, come back later

im currently in the process of changing my website, if your interested in seeing more work feel free to drop me an email.

hana_stevenson@yahoo.co.uk

Contact

I'm available for freelance work

First Name:

Last Name:

E-Mail:

Message:

↪ Send

⭐ This online form is simple yet effective, and reinforces (in the green box) that the designer is "available for freelance work."

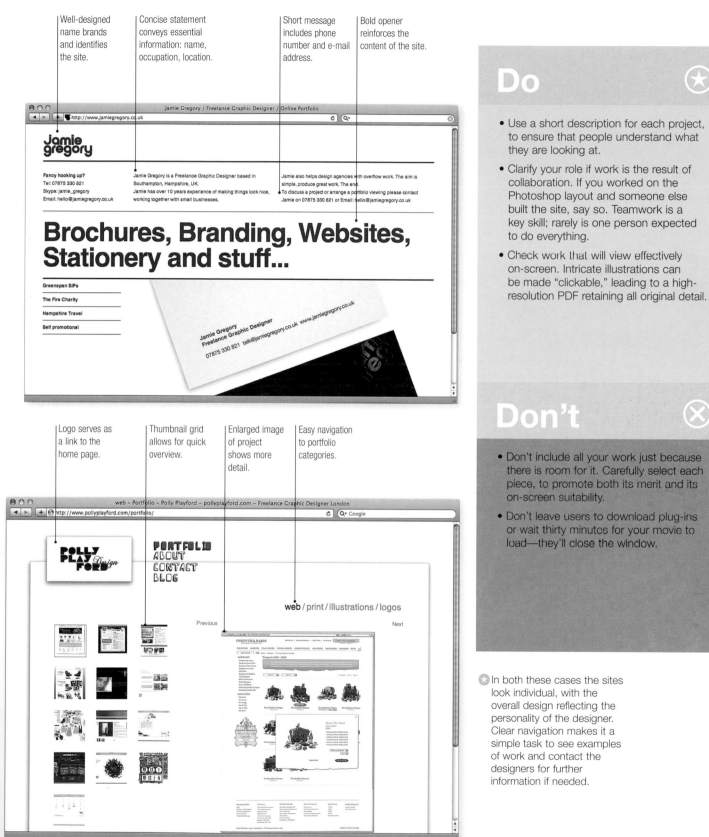

Well-designed name brands and identifies the site.

Concise statement conveys essential information: name, occupation, location.

Short message includes phone number and e-mail address.

Bold opener reinforces the content of the site.

Logo serves as a link to the home page.

Thumbnail grid allows for quick overview.

Enlarged image of project shows more detail.

Easy navigation to portfolio categories.

Do ⭐

- Use a short description for each project, to ensure that people understand what they are looking at.

- Clarify your role if work is the result of collaboration. If you worked on the Photoshop layout and someone else built the site, say so. Teamwork is a key skill; rarely is one person expected to do everything.

- Check work that will view effectively on-screen. Intricate illustrations can be made "clickable," leading to a high-resolution PDF retaining all original detail.

Don't ⊗

- Don't include all your work just because there is room for it. Carefully select each piece, to promote both its merit and its on-screen suitability.

- Don't leave users to download plug-ins or wait thirty minutes for your movie to load—they'll close the window.

⭐ In both these cases the sites look individual, with the overall design reflecting the personality of the designer. Clear navigation makes it a simple task to see examples of work and contact the designers for further information if needed.

Portfolio: Website

• **BUILDING YOUR WEBSITE**
• **CASE STUDY**

If you have the technical skills, build your own portfolio site—not only to give you invaluable experience, but also to enable you to present your work in a unique way. Possibilities are endless, and if you want to move into the realm of digital and online design, this is where you should focus your efforts.

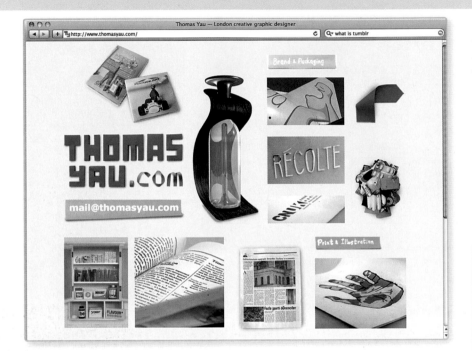

Your online portfolio is a chance to show off your work and make an individual statement. Take time to consider the impact of arriving at the page, as first impressions will last. Do not assume that the user already knows your work—you should give a clear message of who you are and what it is you do. The page title (displayed at the very top of the Web browser) can help with this. In the example left, the title "Thomas Yau—London creative graphic designer" immediately conveys name, location, and area of interest.

Building your website

Express your personality

⭐ Building your own site lets you express your personality and creativity, making your site like no other.

⭐ This site demonstrates both technical skills (having built the site) and an interest in the handmade and detail (having carefully constructed the domain name from paper cutouts).

❗ Create a strong visual impression with your home page, but ensure this is not at the expense of a slow-loading page—visitors will not wait.

Consistency

⭐ Navigation for "forward" and "back" follows the same paper cutout system as established on the home page. Continuity eases navigation and visitors expect consistency.

Attention to detail

⭐ Every aspect of your work, including presentation, may be scrutinized. Care taken in the photograph of a hand holding work demonstrates an understanding of presentation, scale, and attention to detail.

See also →

Choosing and using templates See page 114

Introducing variety to your home page

⭐ Opening with a large or new image is a sure way to get visitors' attention. One of the benefits of building your own site is that you can experiment with programming "random images"—each time a visitor returns, a different image is loaded.

Color theme

⭐ Work with a limited color palette, and one that runs throughout the site and complements the work.

Do ✪

- Decide how to display work for greatest impact. The Thomas Yau example (opposite) uses images on a single page to create a long scrolling effect, whereas Marcus Bastel (left) uses a grid of thumbnail images. Both are effective.

- Pay attention to detail. Ensure professional image quality; use Photoshop to improve, edit, and retouch pictures for on-screen viewing.

- Create a high-impact opening. Thomas Yau (opposite) uses intensely bright and colorful images, which immediately grab your attention. Pace develops into more complex imagery.

- Link to details. Give users the opportunity to view greater detail—both examples here feature clickable images, leading to a higher-resolution image.

- Plan site updates. You must keep content fresh. If work takes a long time to create, hold some back so you can update the site one month after launch.

Don't ✕

- Don't expect people to wait for long flash movies to load. If you have projects with long loading times, warn users by a small caption indicating file size and potential download time. Better still, offer different file sizes to accommodate both those with very slow connections and those on high-speed Internet.

- Don't use a free Web host, unless very highly recommended. Your host will affect loading speed, so it is vital to choose a reputable company.

- Don't include all your work—as iterated throughout this book, be selective.

Case study

Jamie Hearn's website (www.jamiehearn.com) is relatively simple, but it also expresses both his personality and his work. Such sites can be built using any standard Web authoring software (e.g., Adobe Dreamweaver or Microsoft Expression Web). Having built the site, the designer knows how it works; more important, he has full control over updating it when needed.

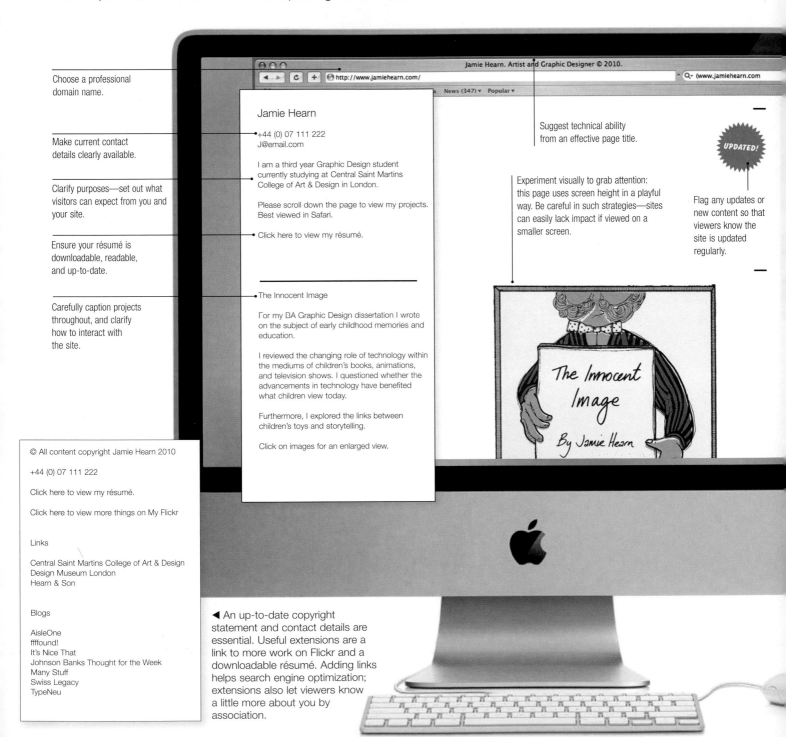

Choose a professional domain name.

Make current contact details clearly available.

Clarify purposes—set out what visitors can expect from you and your site.

Ensure your résumé is downloadable, readable, and up-to-date.

Carefully caption projects throughout, and clarify how to interact with the site.

Suggest technical ability from an effective page title.

Experiment visually to grab attention: this page uses screen height in a playful way. Be careful in such strategies—sites can easily lack impact if viewed on a smaller screen.

UPDATED!

Flag any updates or new content so that viewers know the site is updated regularly.

Jamie Hearn. Artist and Graphic Designer © 2010.

http://www.jamiehearn.com/

News (347) ▼ Popular ▼

Jamie Hearn

+44 (0) 07 111 222
J@email.com

I am a third year Graphic Design student currently studying at Central Saint Martins College of Art & Design in London.

Please scroll down the page to view my projects. Best viewed in Safari.

Click here to view my résumé.

The Innocent Image

For my BA Graphic Design dissertation I wrote on the subject of early childhood memories and education.

I reviewed the changing role of technology within the mediums of children's books, animations, and television shows. I questioned whether the advancements in technology have benefited what children view today.

Furthermore, I explored the links between children's toys and storytelling.

Click on images for an enlarged view.

The Innocent Image
By Jamie Hearn

© All content copyright Jamie Hearn 2010

+44 (0) 07 111 222

Click here to view my résumé.

Click here to view more things on My Flickr

Links

Central Saint Martins College of Art & Design
Design Museum London
Hearn & Son

Blogs

AisleOne
ffffound!
It's Nice That
Johnson Banks Thought for the Week
Many Stuff
Swiss Legacy
TypeNeu

◄ An up-to-date copyright statement and contact details are essential. Useful extensions are a link to more work on Flickr and a downloadable résumé. Adding links helps search engine optimization; extensions also let viewers know a little more about you by association.

Click here to view my résumé.

Buzz Warhol

Intergalactic Avant Garde Superhero.
Click on Buzz for enlarged view.

Use Photoshop to cut out images. This shows attention to detail, foresight of what looks accomplished, and skill in more intricate work.

The Vegtand TR-909

Visual identity for the world most innovative musical instrument.
Click on images for enlarged view.

Bold color and graphic images work well when presented on-screen.

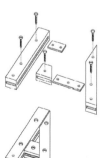

Objectography

I created a typeface from a coherent set of everyday components and illustrated in a information graphic through the medium of posters. I drew inspiration for the layout design from Swiss typograms legend Jan Tschichold.

Instructions for Assembly

Click on images for high resolution PDF whereby zooming in will allow detail to be viewed.

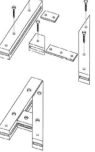

Die Neue Typographie
Jan Tschichold
1928

Pros and cons to website portfolios

⭐ Control over design gives you a unique portfolio.

⭐ If you have requisite knowledge or are prepared to learn, there's almost no limit to what you can do.

⭐ By building your site, you showcase both your work and your Web design skills.

⭐ You will learn multiple skills to do with design, software, Web servers, and more.

❗ This is technically challenging work, especially as your site must appear both current and standards compliant.

❗ Building professional websites is very time consuming; you may have little time to update your site.

❗ It is too easy to get wrapped up in site building and lose the main focus on your work (assuming this is not Web design.)

❗ A nonprofessional-looking site will potentially do more harm than good.

Crucial criteria

Your online portfolio, especially if presented as your website, will be judged on both content and other fundamental factors:

• How easy is it to navigate?

• Does the site load quickly?

• Does the site work on my computer?

• Is work understandable?

• Is work clearly captioned and correctly attributed?

• Does the site, and, therefore, the person behind the site, have a great personality?

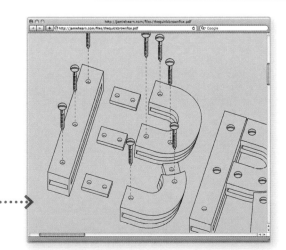

◄ Link to details of pieces. This both shows off work to its best advantage, and demonstrates attention to detail and an understanding of display in digital format.

Portfolio: Blog

- **WHAT TO INCLUDE**
- **CASE STUDY**
- **BUILDING YOUR BLOG**

Thanks to developments within Web publishing, it is now easier than ever to have an online presence. Blogs are one of the simplest means of entry, but it is a difficult task to create something that is well designed, written, and presented. You will have to work very hard to stand out from the crowd.

A blog (contraction of the term *Web log*) is essentially a website. The true definition of a blog is difficult to pin down, as it is a changing system. Many think of blogs as online diaries or journals; however, they can more closely resemble traditional websites. Many blog publishing systems give options to include or exclude user comments, so ultimately you have as much control over a blog as you do over a regular website.

What to include

Because it is relatively easy to set up a blog, it can be all too easy not to scrutinize the content. A blog can be like writing a personal diary, and, as such, it is easy not to take care with the grammar, style of writing, and spelling. However, a blog is for public viewing, and that includes potential employers. Carefully consider the following points and draw up a plan.

Content
- What will the content be?
- Is my content in a ready-to-use format (scanned, retouched)? If not, how will I prepare content?
- How will content be categorized?
- How might categories grow in the near future, and will this fit with the overall blog scheme?

Design
- Have I found a suitable template or blog theme?

Maintenance
- How often will I update my blog?
- Is my update schedule realistic?

Technical
- Is my domain name available?
- Can I afford a suitable host?
- Do I have the technical skills to achieve what I want?

Tone
- Will your blog be a hard-sell portfolio of your work, or something a little more quirky and more about your personality and interests? Much depends on the clients you wish to pitch at, and the visitors you hope to attract.

See also ⟶

Choosing and using templates See page 114

Pros and cons

⭐ Blogs are simple to update.

⭐ Blogs are searchable.

⭐ It is easy to add media such as video.

⭐ Many websites use software based on or similar to blogs, so being able to manage a blog is a useful skill.

⭐ Accomplished blogs can generate substantial interest and many followers.

❗ Design parameters are usually restrictive.

❗ Alteration of core function and design is technically challenging.

❗ You may need regular updates from your blog software provider to keep your software up-to-date.

⭐ Swiss Miss (www.swiss-miss.com) was started in 2005 as a personal archive and has become one of the most successful design blogs. Swiss Miss, aka Tina Roth Eisenberg, is now using the reputable name of her blog as the name of her successful design company. Although not specifically a portfolio, the site undoubtedly brings in publicity and work for the studio, and so serves the same function.

Case study

A clear design with strong visuals on the opening page creates impact.
Your blog needs to be immediately clear to understand.

Choose a professional domain name.

Clarify purposes—what visitors can expect from you and your site.

Establish a clear and user-friendly navigation structure. Consider categorization and labeling very carefully.

The services page presents a well-written and clear statement outlining exactly the services offered.

⭐ Kerry Nehil's portfolio site (www.kerrynehil.com) is built using WordPress (see page 108). A strong home page with obvious visual impact leads to specific projects.

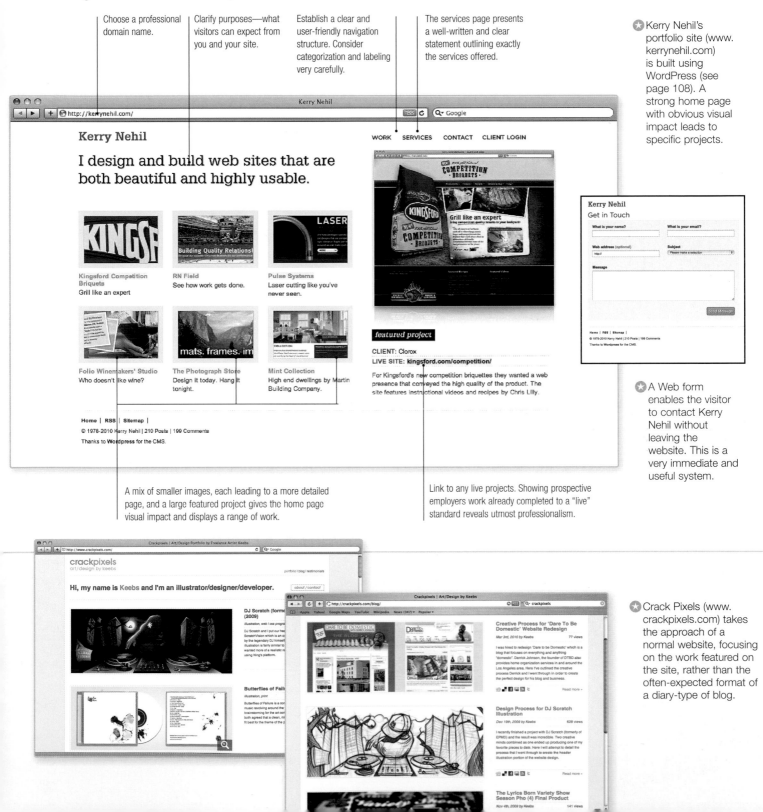

A mix of smaller images, each leading to a more detailed page, and a large featured project gives the home page visual impact and displays a range of work.

Link to any live projects. Showing prospective employers work already completed to a "live" standard reveals utmost professionalism.

⭐ A Web form enables the visitor to contact Kerry Nehil without leaving the website. This is a very immediate and useful system.

⭐ Crack Pixels (www.crackpixels.com) takes the approach of a normal website, focusing on the work featured on the site, rather than the often-expected format of a diary-type of blog.

Building your blog

There are many free and paid-for systems available to help you build a blog, so it is important that you choose the appropriate one. Make sure you research the full range of options available to you at the time.

⭐ WordPress is an open-source self-publishing system, created to "enhance the typography of everyday writing."

In many ways, your choice of platform/system for building your blog or website is similar to choice of presentation for your portfolio, whether in A3, A2, or constructed box format. It depends on what you are trying to convey and who you are pitching to.

At the time of writing, WordPress is the most popular blogging platform. There are two different options: WordPress.com and WordPress.org (see Pros and cons below for a comparison).

Pros and cons: WordPress

⭐ WordPress is a great choice, for both a regular blog and a portfolio site. It makes content publishing easy, and because of its popularity there are many plug-ins and extensions.

⭐ You can re-theme WordPress using hundreds of free or premium (paid for) themes. There are many free tutorials for setting up a blog; just search online.

⭐ There are many competing products and services available, and almost monthly a new service aimed at getting you and your work online is launched.

❗ With WordPress.com, you have limited design options for customization; instead, access WordPress.org to download the latest version. You will need a Web host for installation.

What to consider

• Will the platform accommodate your type of work? If video is what you do, there's little point in using a system that makes it difficult to upload video.

• Are there restrictions in place? For example, some hosted systems deter you from uploading more than a certain number of images; if you upload more, you have to pay.

• Do you have enough technical knowledge to be able to complete the website?

• Are templates, extensions, and plug-ins available to use, to extend the site's capabilities?

• Is there enough online/off-line support to enable you to set up the site you want to set up?

• Are there hidden or future costs to consider?

Pros and cons: Joomla

⭐ This is a large community of experts who often offer free advice and help.

⭐ Many themes, extensions, and plug-ins are available allowing you to extend core functionality.

❗ It requires a certain amount of knowledge to set up and install.

❗ Updating is required to keep your version current.

⭐ Joomla (www.joomla.org) is another open-source content management system. Although not as popular as WordPress, it has hundreds of thousands of users.

⭐ Joomla can be re-skinned, giving your site a different appearance, as these two examples demonstrate.

⭐ A content management system such as Joomla makes it easy for you to update your site.

Pros and cons: Tumblr

⭐ Little or no coding is required.

⭐ Posting text, images, and video is free.

⭐ Setup is free.

❗ This is a relatively new system, and not as widely used as WordPress, so there is not the same level of community support.

❗ The system is not built to deal with specific needs of creatives, though it is customizable to some extent.

⭐ Tumblr (www.tumblr.com) is the newest of the systems covered here, and well worth a look. If you want to do as little coding as possible, this may well be your best option.

⭐ As demonstrated by these two examples, Tumblr sites can look totally different from one another.

⭐ Choose from the range of prebuilt themes, or code your own.

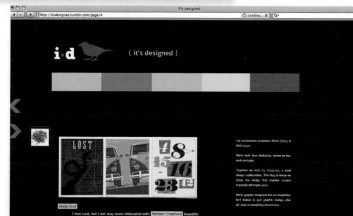

Portfolio: Network

If you don't want to build your own site, or if you want another avenue of exposure, consider the growing number of sites where you can upload your work. Being part of a network can bring increased exposure and enable your work to reach a global audience. Many designers have work featured on both their own site and a network site.

• **BUILDING YOUR NETWORK**
• **CASE STUDY**

Pros and cons

⭐ You can reach a much wider audience than you would probably otherwise find.

⭐ Referrals may lead to increased exposure or work.

⭐ Membership is often free, and easy to set up.

⭐ Many sites have features that you would never be able to build yourself.

❗ Large networks have thousands, if not hundreds of thousands, of members, so it is difficult to stand out.

❗ Often networks have statistics available; visitors may know if others rate your work poorly, as well as highly.

❗ Many network sites do not let you modify the design, which limits customization possibilities. As a result everyone's piece is on a level playing field and visitors look only at the work, not at the website around the work.

❗ Advertising can clutter work views, but since this is how most network sites earn money, you just have to live with it.

❗ Many people use such websites for "inspiration," and others may draw reference and inspiration from your work. This is the case whenever you post pieces online but, because of the nature of networks, it's more likely to happen here.

Essentially social network portfolio sites offer you the facility to upload work and create professional relationships between categories of work and individuals within the network. Sites often have additional features, such as peer-group feedback, and, if successful, they develop into large-scale communities of like-minded individuals.

Building your network

Two of the most popular portfolio sites are Behance.net and Deviantart.com. These sites offer you the opportunity of reaching out to millions of potential visitors, some of whom may be potential clients. Even if you already have a website of your own, being part of such a network can bring enormous benefit and promotion, and, as joining is free in most cases, you have little to lose by signing up. That said, apply the golden rules of keeping pages up-to-date and carefully considering which work to include.

⭐ Behance.net lets you build your portfolio for free and receives millions of visits. By being part of the network you get the chance of being spotted. A unique Web address allows you to send potential employers a link to your portfolio.

Browse

Browse

Deviations
Prints Shop
T-Shirts & Gear
Groups

Category

Digital Art
Photography
Traditional Art
Film & Animation
Contests
Customization
Artisan Crafts

Popular   Newest

Most popular deviations submitted in the **last 8 hours**

commission-lillumsama
In Traditional Art

Blutrot
In Photography

⭐ With more than 11 million members, Deviantart is another huge community you can join. A comprehensive structure, including photography, movies, and art, enables users to organize their own portfolios.

JOIN DEVIANTART NOW!

Join the largest art community in the world! Membership is FREE to share and sell your artwork, start your Art Collection and track your favorite artists!

Choose a username!

yournamehere   .deviantart.com

Join!

Join Now Buy deviantWEAR Advertise Here

Do ⭐

- Research the most suitable and the specialty networks.

- Consider joining a smaller community for larger exposure; in a huge network, you may struggle to be seen. It depends on your work and the network.

- Consider signing up with more than one network, to represent the different aspects of your work.

- Keep your contact details up-to-date.

- Keep your work up-to-date, uploading fresh work as it is available.

- Join in any online feedback. Often those who participate get increased exposure.

- Consider any links to networks such as Facebook and Flickr. Such links can be useful, but make sure the content and photos are appropriate for a future employer.

⭐ Signing up is a quick and easy process, facilitated by the membership form (above).
⭐ If your work is new or proves to be popular, it might be featured on the Deviantart home page.
⭐ Thumbnail images link through to further details and profiles.

Don't ⊗

- Don't be tempted to upload all your work. As stressed throughout this book, be selective.

- Don't forget that thousands may see your images. Take care in your photography and aim for perfection.

Case study

Ever growing in popularity, Behance is a great place to showcase work. Here is a selection of work by one designer.

Upload multiple "albums" of work, though format and image size is often beyond your control.

Advertising is usually how network sites make money; unfortunately, you have to live with this.

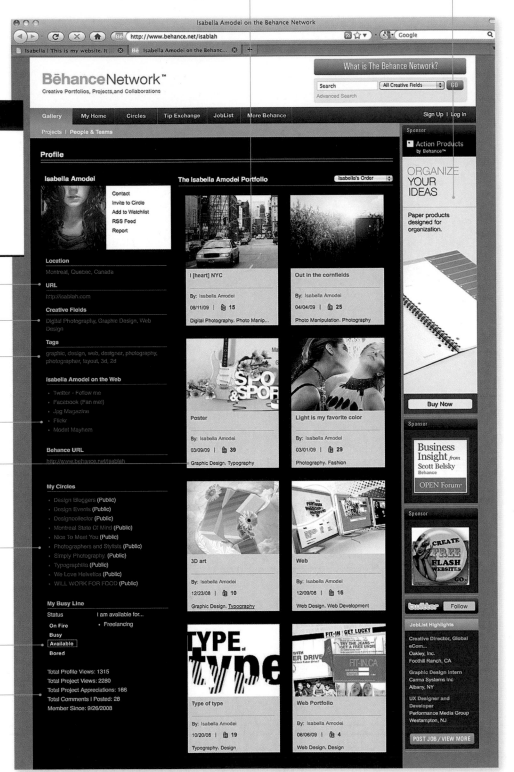

Link to your own website.

Categorize and promote your areas of work and interest.

Specify tags so your work gets found in network searches.

Link to other places where you can be found online.

Take care in categorizing your work, so that others will find it more easily.

Link to others to contextualize your work. Ideally others will then reciprocate, increasing your exposure.

Clarify that you are available for work, and what sort of work.

Be aware of network publicity—many make information such as the popularity of your work available to everyone.

⭐ By offering job listings and other useful information, Behance encourages users to make repeat visits to the site, and more visitors helps your work get more exposure.

Some popular options

As with all things online, space changes frequently. At the time of writing, some of the most popular network sites you can join include behance.net and deviantart.com (see pages 110–111). There are other options:

• Flickr—this is a widely used site to upload images. Extend your portfolio by linking to your Flickr page.

• LinkedIn—this is a professional business networking site, not specifically a place to upload your work, but an important online tool.

• MySpace—this can also be customized to include your own portfolio and images.

Other media

The Web has revolutionized how we work and how we present work, and it is an ever-evolving field. If the adage "A picture is worth a thousand words" is true, video is worth considerably more, and is playing an increasingly important role in the presentation of creative work.

⭐ At the time of writing, the two most popular websites to upload video to are www.youtube.com and www.vimeo.com. In both cases you must register for a free account; then you can upload your work.

⭐ The potential for creatives is huge. Packaging designers can showcase work in 3D, advertisers can upload short commercials, and animators can create their own movies.

⭐ With the availability of high-definition video cameras at affordable prices, combined with software to edit footage, it has never been easier to get film, video, and animations seen.

⭐ Through both YouTube and Vimeo, a simple piece of Web code, once pasted into your own site, feeds your footage into your website. Not only does this help set your website apart from others, but it is another opportunity to increase your number of website visitors.

Choosing and using templates

Unless you are specializing in Web design, you may find it a challenge to build a site or blog that reflects the quality of your non-Web work. You may find templates a suitable option.

Web templates are predesigned Web pages or websites. There are thousands to choose from, ranging from simple HTML to more complex blog themes and Flash photo galleries. Templates minimize what you need to know about programming and designing for the Web.

You will find both premium and free templates. Premium templates tend to come with source files and are better documented. Carefully read any license agreements; some conditions stipulate that you credit the template author.

Pitching yourself as a Web designer? Don't use a prebuilt template! If your skills are up to it, create your own and make it available to others to download.

Designing your own templates
If you are skillful enough at Web design, consider designing your own templates for uploading onto sites such as ThemeForest. Not only can you earn money from sharing your designs, but you can also provide great exposure for your work.

You may find similar template "stores" for your specialty. Many designers earn an income by designing corporate identities, business cards, PowerPoint presentations, brochures, and more. As well as the income, you will gain valuable client-based feedback on your work.

How to find templates
Spend a half hour online searching for "Web template," "premium template," and "HTML template"—you will find hundreds of resources. Always read license agreements and the terms and conditions of use.

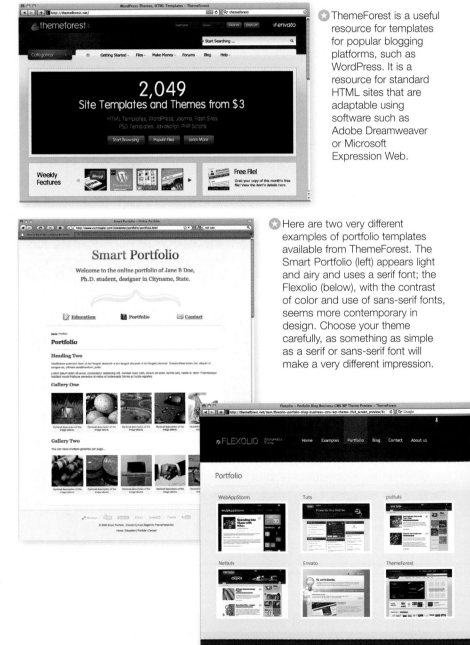

★ ThemeForest is a useful resource for templates for popular blogging platforms, such as WordPress. It is a resource for standard HTML sites that are adaptable using software such as Adobe Dreamweaver or Microsoft Expression Web.

★ Here are two very different examples of portfolio templates available from ThemeForest. The Smart Portfolio (left) appears light and airy and uses a serif font; the Flexolio (below), with the contrast of color and use of sans-serif fonts, seems more contemporary in design. Choose your theme carefully, as something as simple as a serif or sans-serif font will make a very different impression.

What software to use

There are many applications that can be used to create websites. Two of the most popular are Adobe Dreamweaver and Microsoft Expression Web. Both require you to deal with design and programming issues, but they are essential tools of the online design field. There are also several cheaper options, as well as free "open-source" applications. Get searching online!

Portfolio creators

A number of online portfolio creators have appeared alongside "traditional" software options. Online creators target those who do not want (or know how) to build a "traditional" website but who want to publish an online portfolio.

Less flexible than building your own site, this option may appeal to those not wanting to invest time learning Web design and development. At the time of writing, Carbonmade.com is a more popular option.

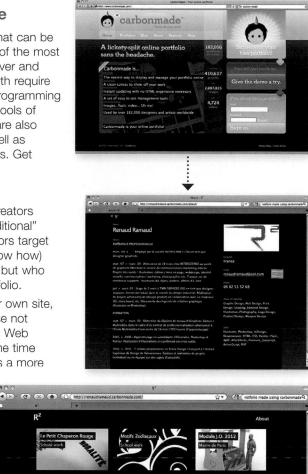

⭐ The work of Renaud Ramaud (renaudramaud. carbonmade.com) is presented in a clear format, in part thanks to the structure of Carbonmade. The portfolio is easy to navigate and work is professionally presented.

❗ Web designers would be expected not to use a system such as Carbonmade.

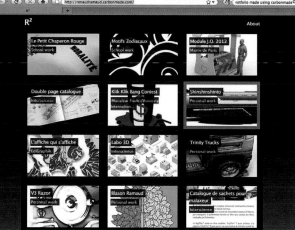

⭐ Another popular source of templates is www. templatemonster.com. This website contains thousands of templates to purchase. Each one is different, and designed by a member of the in-house Template Monster team.

Get your portfolio noticed

Assuming you have built yourself a website, set up a blog, or got your work on portfolio networks, how do you make sure it is seen, and by the right people?

There is no instant solution to getting your portfolio found by people. Strong content and a well-designed and easy-to-navigate website is a very positive start, but it is only the start.

Search engines
⭐ Most websites rely on search engines for traffic. A complex system of analysis is used by search engines, and one important factor affecting this is keywords. You must understand keywords for your site. The Google page https://adwords.google.com/select/KeywordToolExternal will help. Search online for SEO (search engine optimization) for a huge amount of information.

Keep content fresh
⭐ Search engines prefer regularly updated sites, as do site users—these are two reasons to keep your site updated on a regular basis.

Keep it unique
⭐ If your site has strong and unique content, not only will visitors value it, but you may find other sites and bloggers linking to you and writing about your work.

Keep in contact
⭐ A positive strategy is to run a mailing list. This can be easily done with a simple Web form on your site. Decide on frequency; perhaps once a month e-mail subscribers news and updates about your work.

Be social
⭐ Although it may be inadvisable to link from your website to your Facebook profile, depending on content and image, there may be no harm in using the likes of Facebook, Twitter, Flickr, and other social networks. Place a link to your website in your profile and encourage friends and followers to visit your site.

Give it away
⭐ Many sites encourage repeat users and referrals from other sites by giving things away. If you are an illustrator, you could, for example, prepare a different screen saver every month and make this available for downloading.

Do what you excel at
⭐ Advertisers could make a viral ad, and print designers could prepare a low-budget flyer. Put your mind to it and think of ways you can market your own website using services and skills.

Splash pages are a no-go
❗ All the rage a few years ago, opening splash pages and Flash animations are to be avoided if you are an individual wanting to get seen. They harm your search engine chances and generally annoy visitors.

Creating a one-page presence

If you have neither the time nor the knowledge to put together a full website, try a cleverly designed single-page site—it's better than nothing.

This site (www.isablah.com) shows how you can link to other resources such as your portfolio on Behance (see Network, page 110) or your LinkedIn profile.

Make a clear call to action, such as "hire me."

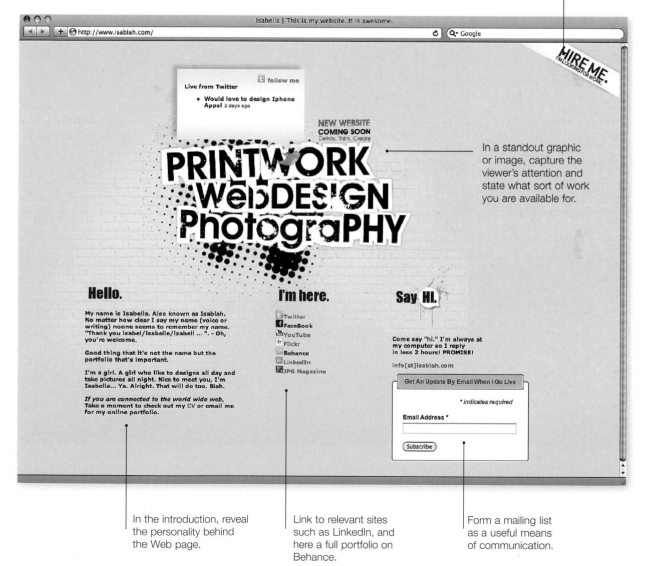

In a standout graphic or image, capture the viewer's attention and state what sort of work you are available for.

In the introduction, reveal the personality behind the Web page.

Link to relevant sites such as LinkedIn, and here a full portfolio on Behance.

Form a mailing list as a useful means of communication.

promoting yourself

Even if you are not comfortable with the idea of promoting yourself, you will have to take a deep breath and get on with it. Your main promotional tool is your portfolio, and as a next step it must reach the right people. Regardless of destination and chosen field, at some point you will need a cover letter and a résumé expanded in digital format. Graphic designers tend to avoid the standard format Word résumé; instead, they aim for a unique document that looks professional and reads well.

This chapter gives tips to get you started and examples to inspire you. It examines additional elements for an accomplished portfolio and considers self-promotion for a young designer. The job search is just the beginning: ask yourself what kind of a job you want, or whether you would prefer to start off on your own. These daunting decisions can become a rewarding exercise in self-discovery and the start of a continual search.

chapter

A career in art and design is fluid—a mix
of working both for yourself and for others.
Your career may twist and turn in response
to a changing environment, and requisite
skills for independent navigation are
explained in the following pages.

Writing your résumé

A good résumé should serve as a well-stated summary of your experience and skills as they relate to the job for which you are applying. The résumé should show your ability to handle responsibility and challenge. It is important to keep in mind that a company often receives scores of applicants. Résumés are scanned in a matter of seconds, so the ability to stand out through a page design that highlights key areas is pivotal for advancing to the next stage.

A lot of available advice is not appropriate for résumés in the creative sector, so beware of what you find from search engines about magic formulas. In graphic design, clarity of information combined with a simple aesthetic is paramount.

What to include
Start with your name, address, and current contact details at the top of the page. Clarify how you wish to be contacted. Include a short profile, incorporating an outline of work experience and key design skills to fit the job.

1 Personal details
You must of course include your contact details, cell phone, e-mail, and so on. According to U.S. and European employment laws you need not include date of birth, gender, disability, ethnic origin, or marital status.

2 Personal statement
A personal statement is mandatory. Include one that fits the relevant industry, and keep it short, clarifying your aims. See page 122 for further information.

3 Education and qualifications
Date and list education and qualifications in reverse chronological order, including institutions. Keep information short and relevant.

4 Work experience
Until you have been employed for some years, you should include under this heading any projects with external employers, for example, any real-life projects completed at college, and any exhibitions or community projects. List your internships, no matter how brief, giving accurate dates, details of the company, and your contributions while you were there. You may also want to elaborate on the main skills you developed and anything new that you learned.

5 Other skills
Refer to other achievements not covered elsewhere, such as languages, IT skills, and craft skills. You could have a titled section on key skills and/or software skills, continually updated as your abilities develop—employers could be trying to fill a gap in their studio and your list may provide the right criteria.

6 Interests and hobbies
Interests and hobbies are optional, but can give a valuable insight into your character and prove to be a talking point in an interview. Every designer could list "going to exhibitions" and "watching films"; consider mentioning instead a club you have started or joined, a particular connection to another country and its culture, or a personal collection of memorabilia.

7 Reference details
The commonly used phrase is "References available on request." Don't list referees at this point; give details when needed, and then let the referees know that they may be contacted.

Key terms

A résumé is a summary of work experience and education, used for a job application.

A cover letter is a letter that accompanies your résumé, addressed to an interviewer.

A reference letter is a formal letter of recommendation, written not by you but by someone who knows you professionally. It is addressed to a potential employer by a referee.

A referee is a person who can recommend you and write a reference letter in a professional capacity. A friend does not write this! You may ask a teacher or someone who knows you in an academic capacity; however, this carries less weight than a professional recommendation.

A personal statement is the short paragraph that starts a résumé. You may have used one on applications to colleges and drafted one on leaving school. For graphic design this is less important than a portfolio—your visual personal statement.

Make it memorable

★ This résumé works both as a PDF and as a printed letter. The use of dynamic color on the first page is memorable, and the first name only in display type is confident design.

Ease of use

★ The text is laid out in a clear two-column format so that the reader can scan it. The student can also make changes or additions easily, without having to redesign the page.

Keep it relevant

❗ Don't devote too much space to employment history, as the jobs are not related to graphic design. You can include any jobs—indeed, they show employability and motivation, and can provide evidence of other skills such as organization and taking responsibility—but be careful of the weighting you give them. It is best to make the most of your work experience and internships.

helen.

helen.

www.iamhelen.co.uk
helen@hotmail.co.uk
+00 11122223

technical skills

OS X Mac Literate:
Adobe InDesign / Photoshop / Illustrator

Knowledge of:
Adobe Dreamweaver / ImageReady / AfterEffects
Quark Xpress / Microsoft Office

education / qualifications

The Arts Institute at Bournemouth 2004–2007
BA (Hons) Graphic Design 2:1

Ravensbourne College of Design and Communication 2003–2004
(BTEC) Diploma in Foundation Studies Art and Design Pass

work experience

May Design /
August 2007–September 2007 4 The Street, London SEE 4DD

An insightful period of time where I gained valuable knowledge of the industry, as well as experience of running the studio. I contributed to a number of exciting briefs, generating initial ideas, as well as developing a design that has been selected for print.

Trade Magazine /
August 2007 6th Floor House, Roberta Street, London SEE 4DA

A worthwhile experience working as an in-house graphic designer, designing ads for clients. The role relied upon team work between designers and sales personnel, and taught me the importance of communication and self motivation, especially when a deadline is approaching.

FFFF Advertising /
January 2007–July 2007 3rd Floor House, The Street, London SGG 4DA

A valuable period of time which allowed me to gain an insight into the general running of the organization. This opportunity allowed me to mix with designers and to work alongside them on live briefs.

employment history

August 2006–September 2006 Partner & Co. The House, The Way, London SAG 2AD

Door-to-door fundraising—a team-based, exciting experience involved knocking on doors to gain contributions for charity. This built upon my communication skills and general self-confidence. It encouraged self-motivation in order to hit targets and achieve a bonus, and has taught me the importance of teamwork.

October 2005–June 2006 Stripe, Christchurch Road, Sussex BNN 11G

Sales assistant—providing customer service, dealing with finances, and stock control. Added responsibility to assist and train work-experience employees, which enabled me to take the initiative and develop my communications skills.

February 2002–September 2004 Garden Center, London Road TNN 7XX

Café assistant—working as an active team player to maintain efficiency, and excellent service. I worked under pressure and kept calm in difficult situations for example, when short staffed. I am multiskilled and able to work a variety jobs, such as operating tills, serving customers, food preparation, and cleaning duties.

achievements

Whilst fundraising, my team and I were proud to have achieved first place out of seventeen teams around the UK, in the week commencing 25th August 2006.

I have been practising karate for seven years and have achieved a black belt. This has led to increased confidence, self-control, and self-discipline.

hobbies / interests

I am a passionate, enthusiastic, creative and interested in all areas of design. I gather inspiration from everything and anything.

I am a motivated and organized person who can adapt quickly to change and thrives on new tasks. I enjoy meeting new people and experiencing new things. I am looking for a Graphic Design job into which I can channel all my energy and enthusiasm, in order to do what I love best.

referees

Academic /
Mr. Referee, The Arts Institute, Bournemouth, Wallisdown, Poole, Dorset BH12 5HH. t/07799 8888888

Work /
Mrs. Referee, Partner & Co., The House, The Way, London SAG 2AD. t/ 01144332211

personal details

1175 House Road, London NN5 66J

Date of birth / 1st January 1985

Do ⓦ

- Check for spelling and grammatical errors. Ask someone else to read your résumé.

- Be honest about college dates and times. It is tempting to stretch dates or internship periods, but any form of deceit is not recommended—if discovered, it will put doubt in the mind of the interviewer.

- Read through job ads carefully and stick to what they ask for. If they want three hard copies of your résumé, supply as directed.

- Try to keep within two sides of A4. The only reason to use more is for an academic application, but here you are focusing on getting a job.

- List work chronologically, starting with the most recent.

Don't ⊗

- Don't use a thousand-word academic personal statement. No one has time to read this at interview, though it may be read for a college or grant application.

- Don't attach other letters to the cover letter or résumé. Wait for a job offer and then supply reference letters.

- Don't try to crack jokes, as you don't know the context and they may fall flat.

- Don't complain about previous employers—it is neither the time nor the place.

- Don't give a cell phone number that you no longer use or a Web address that you never check.

- Don't include every single job position, such as dogsitter, since leaving school; list only relevant experience that shows transferable and key skills. In graphics this will be teamwork, time management, organization, self-motivation, and problem-solving, for example.

- Don't exaggerate. Remember that if you say you are a wonderful typographer, your portfolio should show the evidence to back this up. Rely on your portfolio to reveal skills and talent.

Writing a personal statement

A personal statement can act as a summary of you as a graphic designer and the skills you have to offer. Here we take a look at some real student examples. Bear in mind that your statement should be appropriate to your situation, so the following should be used as guidelines only.

1 Be concise yet personal

"I am a student undertaking a year in professional placements before the final year of my degree. Since starting my course, I have developed a passion for information design. This means design that not only looks good aesthetically but also functions to fulfill a purpose. The key for me is visual problem-solving. I am interested in 3D info, such as exhibition design and signage, and have worked in 3D frequently in the past year. I am confident using software as well as traditional craft media. I have done a lot of layout designs using typography and image and I love working with complex information that needs simplifying."

❗ This statement covers all the main points and is informative, but it is too long. Aim for a maximum of three sentences—a good way to work toward this is to write everything you want to say, then reread it and edit it down until it is the right length.

❗ This statement is a little dry and lacks personality. A personal statement should reveal something about you, even if it is that you are straightforward and clear.

2 State your skills rather than purpose

"I am excited, enthusiastic, and passionate about the communication of great ideas. In the belief that great design grows from these ideas, I always try to combine thorough research and a sharp visual awareness with solutions that aim to maintain clarity in both message and aesthetic."

❗ This statement reads well but is more a mission statement than a personal statement of what the designer has to offer.

3 List relevant qualities

"Friendly, open-minded, hardworking, committed, optimistic, good sense of humor, adaptable to new situations, creative, good team player, always striving to achieve the highest standard in everything I do."

❗ A list of the qualities that every applicant should have does show that you understand what is required of you, but lacks anything memorable or different to make you stand out. Make sure that you list only those relevant to you and the role.

4 Let it flow

"A graphic design student who is keen to find an internship/placement in a related field. Creative, imaginative, reliable, and prompt. Worked as an intern last summer and gained a good understanding of what is required of a graphic designer. Able to work on own initiative or as part of a team and can deal with administrative duties competently."

⭐ Talking about yourself in the third person can be a way around the over-use of "I."

⭐ This example reads well, and so sounds natural rather than forced, making all the main points succinctly.

Designing your résumé

In designing your résumé, you should be better qualified than anyone! However, you must be objective and choose the best ideas to communicate who you are and what you want to do. Examples below illustrate different directions.

1 Keep it simple and organized

Use lists or short sentences; avoid long paragraphs. Edit work to one page.

2 Small, bold headings to organize content

Vary typography for a hierarchy that leads the reader in. Once you have input information, spend time on typographic detail. This will make a major difference to the overall impression.

3 Appropriate fonts

Your interviewer may be a type purist, especially if you are targeting book and magazine design. Be wary of screen fonts for your résumé; instead, choose those designed to be read in print. The reverse applies, of course: in converting to PDF format, to be read on-screen, you may want to redesign it for screen format. Make sure that your chosen font works well on-screen and the letterforms do not drop out (or fade) as some delicate print fonts will do. See online information from Ellen Lupton (www.thinkingwithtypes.com, http://www.papress.com/other/thinkingwithtype/index.htm).

4 Make it digital

For online submissions, keep your résumé simple, check that it is legible, and ensure that all users can open it. The file size should be small enough so that it is easy to e-mail and open. Some recruiters will request a template filled in online—use skills-related key words such as *organized* and *teamwork*. These database forms are only a tool to help search for freelancers. Try to include a link to your real résumé.

The straightforward approach

★ The résumé top left has all the essential information clearly and stylishly presented.

..........➤

Less is more

★ This is an example of minimal text where the content speaks for itself. The résumé acts as an endorsement of the standard of his work. It takes only a few seconds to read, too, and is graphically pleasing.

Résumé example: Mike Andrews

Mike Andrews
Graphic Designer

07999 9999999

mike@cyberspace.co.uk

1A The Wood Road
Edinburgh
TQQ 88B

University College Falmouth – *2006-2009*
First Class BA (Hons) – Graphic Design

Exeter College – *2005-2006*
Art Foundation ABC Diploma

A Levels – *2003-2005*
Fine Art – A
Media Studies – A
English Literature – B
History AS - C

GCSEs – *1999-2005*
1 A*, 3 As, 5 Bs, 1 C

Skills
Competent using a range of software, particularly InDesign, Illustrator, Photoshop, and Dreamweaver. I'm also comfortable using CSS and HTML, and have a basic understanding of Premiere and Flash.

2008
Design Consultancy, London
4-week placement

During my second year I managed to get a month-long placement at Design, a large branding and retail design studio n London. I gained invaluable experience working in a large studio on various branding projects. Working at Design gave me a taste of how the industry works in terms of pace and structure and put me in a good position to come back and finish my degree with all guns blazing.

2007-2008
Princess Pavilion, Falmouth
Bar Staff

The main thing I've taken from working at the Princess Pavilion is coping under high pressure situations behind a small bar on nights when the venue is very busy. It also provided an insight into the idiosyncrasies of Cornish culture, playing host to a range of events from traditional men's choir nights to cabaret-style entertainment to up-and-coming Cornish rap.

Personal

Graphic Design is very important to me. It is where I have found that my instincts and intuition are best placed. As well as having attraction toward the implementation of typography and image, I am also very interested in the social context of design and the influence we can have on societies and cultures, and vice versa. I think it is an inquisitive and analytic nature that draws me toward the industry—a need to find out how and why, to go deeper than just the aesthetic—and I think this is an integral part of design, informing the way something looks rather than remaining separate from it. I am interested in what graphic design can do for people, whether it's a clear signage system that prevents people from getting lost, or something that evokes emotion in people, I believe it is an influential set of communication tools that a graphic designer has at their disposal, and we should be aware of how we use them.

Résumé example: Jimmy Tilley

```
JIMMY TILLEY: RÉSUMÉ

DESIGN EMPLOYMENT HISTORY:
FULL TIME@ THE FARM (08-09.2005, 01-04-2006)
WORK PLACEMENT@ JOHNSON BANKS (10-12.2005)
WORK PLACEMENT@ COLEY PORTER BELL (06.2004)

EDUCATION:
FIRST-CLASS HONS BA GRAPHIC DESIGN
(KINGSTON UNIVERSITY, 06.200)
FOUNDATION IN ART & DESIGN
(KINGSTON UNIVERSITY, 06.2002)
4 A-LEVELS/9 GCSES
(HAMPTON SCHOOL, 06.2001)

APPLICATIONS:
ILLUSTRATOR, PHOTOSHOP, INDESIGN, AND
QUARKXPRESS

ACHIEVEMENTS:
2005 RSA DESIGN DIRECTIONS AWARDS WINNER
(VOTING BY DESIGN)
2005 D&AD STUDENT AWARDS COMMENDATION
(APPLIED GRAPHIC DESIGN)
2005 D&AD "BEST NEW BLOOD" AWARD WINNER
2005 WORK PRINTED IN DESIGN WEEK AND
CREATIVE REVIEW

EMAIL: jimbo@ema11.co.uk
Mobile: 077775087
Home: 012234567
```

Add detail

⭐ This candidate has had lots of short internships. He has been honest about the dates and laid it all out in detail using rules and proficient typography. For the finishing touch he has also included some reduced-down samples of work.

Reading between the lines

⭐ This is the typical content of someone who has been out of college for a few years. The employment details show a career path. Designers will try out different fields before they decide on one area.

⭐ This résumé stands out as a good example of using the full potential of a page, including playful photography, mini page layouts, and full dates of employment. It makes full use of an A4 format.

No need for a photo

⚠ Although this résumé features a photo, you should not attach one since your job will not include modeling or acting. You won't want to be judged on your appearance; instead maintain focus on skills and experience.

5 Columns create dynamic space

Dividing information by grids will help create vertical space. Horizontal rules or graphic elements produce a document that is pleasing to look at and a pleasure to read. The standard A4 format allows for a well-printed résumé. Remember, though, that landscape format might be more appropriate for interactive designers and for digital format.

6 Illustrate if appropriate

Many creatives struggle with a type-only résumé, feeling the urge to illustrate their work. Graphic designers could insert a few samples. This kind of document is particularly effective for fashion (see the Creative Living website, http://www. careers-creative-living.co.uk/cv_gallery).

7 Brand yourself

You can design a complete visual identity for self-promotional items: your job applications, your site, even your portfolio label. The illustration here has a good sense of humor in the photos and shows an aptitude for type and visual jokes. The designer has created his own brand—perfect for a magazine freelancer.

8 Is it legible?

Make sure that you can e-mail a résumé easily and that it remains legible, including illustrations. An illegible document is a nonstarter; don't get carried away. Although photocopying is no longer common, ensure that it can be read if photocopied or even faxed. Yes, people still use fax machines!

Design should create clarity

This example features strong layout and confident use of vocabulary. Well-designed sections help the reader sift through the information, however, improvements can be made with regard to content.

At a glance, this student stands out as having been busy with work experience while being at college. This indicates her commitment and ability to juggle tasks.

Keep details up-to-date

Keep your résumé fresh by updating this information regularly and, most important, removing old material.

Consider the reader

Landscape format is screen-friendly, but not so good for printing out because of default page settings. Check your résumé on different platforms, i.e., on a PC, then on a Mac, and then on a personal device such as an iPhone.

Background colors should be used with care, as they may affect readability if printed out. Print it yourself and check it thoroughly.

This personal statement is full of interesting information but is too long. Try to find shorter ways of saying the same thing.

Put education in reverse chronological order, starting with the most recent. Your current college is more important and relevant than the school you attended.

List what you have done. Show that you have tried a few different approaches. Often at interview these become talking points, as they set you aside from others. When students have similar academic profiles, employers look for something that sets you apart.

As much as possible, put interesting, relevant, and varied work placements and employment at the top. Keep casual work such as bar jobs and waitressing in a less prominent position, or even leave them out if you have enough internships to fill the space. Include dates.

Margot Bowman
+447788222222
1810 Down Road, N13 HH3
mb@googlemail.com
www.margotbowman.blogspot.com

I'm currently studying Graphic Design BA (Hons) at Central St Martins and I'm passionate about visual communication.

Initially I thought I wanted to work in fashion, and previously I was an intern at Plastique magazine and worked under various stylists, and Net-a-porter.com marketing team. I think I was drawn to fashion because for me it's always been the most immediate form of visual communication, and my interest in it still runs deep.

However, this year I have spent more time focusing on telling my own visual narrative with fanzines that were stocked in Selfridges' stores. These zines are an assimilation of short fiction stories that I write and then add my own photography and illustration to them.

One of the most exciting projects I worked on this year was Sunshine. We set ourselves the challenge of informing people about the impending climate crisis through a free paper that would actually inspire and interest people. This is probably the biggest narrative I have ever worked on but I fully enjoyed the challenge of making it palatable and telling a tired story in a new way.

As well as the above I have been taking part in an interest group. This has allowed me to expand my understanding of the kind of environment I am a part of and the role I have as a designer and as a citizen within it. This area of thinking is one I find increasingly relevant and exciting, and I plan to develop my interest throughout the course.

Education

South Hampstead High School
GCSEs
English, Science, Art, History, Maths

A-Levels
Physics (AS) C
History of Art B
English A
Art A

Camberwell College of Art & Design
2007–2008
Foundation Degree Art and Design Merit

Central St. Martins London
2008–present
BA (Hons) Graphic Design

Skills & Qualifications

Working knowledge of Adobe software (Photoshop, Illustrator, Flash, InDesign)

Basic knowledge of bookbinding

Bronze Duke of Edinburgh Award

Skills & Qualifications

Komokino Casting
Assistant for show

Mindshare
Invention team design and concept intern

Here Comes the Sun
Editorial assistant, writer, and concept development

See Studio
Design intern working on the 100 Magazine & Crystallized

Tamara Cincik
Fashion stylist
Stylist assistant

Rubbish Magazine
The daily paper at LFW, Spring '08

Plastique Publishing
Fashion intern

Deal Real Records
Producing promotional material, running shop, and managing stock

Net–a–Porter.com
Marketing intern and then paid temporary team member

Employment History

Mariano Vivanco
T-shirt & Logo Design for Team Vivanco

Sunday Times Style Magazine
Assistant to Jessica Brinton. This includes covering parties, trend spotting and recently attending the opening the Mazagan Hotel is Morocco on behalf of Jessica. 2008 to present

Le Marche Du Quartier
Part of the Borough Market team on Saturday selling high-end French produce. 2009 to present

Jodie Harsh
P.A. to Jodie over a summer
Organising Circus & financial paper work

Arsenal
Waitress at the season ticket holders restaurant at Emirates

Club nights
Since 2007 I have been running club nights for charitable causes

The How Fridays at The Macbeth
Where Mod meets Modern (Northern Soul, Ska & Dubstep)

Bathtime Passing Clouds
One-off fundraising party for Climate Rush with live performances from Crystal Fighters

Writing your cover letter

In addition to a résumé you may need a cover letter (most of the time your "letter" will be an e-mail but the term is used here to mean a document introducing a résumé, regardless of how it is sent). This can be straightforward—don't go overboard on design, as you will need to tweak the letter for each job application. This is the chance to relate skills to a chosen role. As a summary of skills and achievements, your résumé may cover common ground, so the letter needs to draw in the interviewer. Don't write a stiff business letter; approach this person with respect, not awe.

Sending a letter on spec

Address the letter to the right person. Call the company and ask for the name of the person who recruits designers. Don't address your letter "To whom it may concern."

If you have heard that an agency is hiring but not advertising, say how you obtained this information and why you think you would fit the role.

Replying to a job ad

Start with a sentence saying how you learned of the vacancy and which position you are applying for. Next add a short paragraph about yourself and explain why you think your skills would fit this job. Refer to what you are doing now, but briefly—your résumé will give more information.

Specify the aspects that attract you to the company and the contribution you would hope to make. Finish by affirming that you are available for interview and by thanking the company for the time taken in considering your application.

Cover letter as part of your brand

Consider how you appear to the viewer—the first impression is everything. This example of stationery is trimmed with fur, and there is a cat bell on the business card. In the wrong context, it could be excessive or inappropriate, but in this instance, it was accurately targeted and the candidate got the job.

How to write a successful cover letter

▼ **Give the right impression**

⭐ Having a positive attitude toward the opportunity shows that you will be useful in a busy office and contribute to the team.

Dear John Smith

I am currently a second year student on the Graphic Design course at Anytown University. I am hoping to be considered for an unpaid internship, or a placement, or even some freelance work. I had noticed the post on the virtual blackboard a few weeks back and was hoping I haven't missed a great opportunity!
Who am I? I am Tom and I like typography. I also like good advertising and good ideas. I think I have good ideas but would love to see what you think. I mostly work with print. With a friendly and enthusiastic personality, I will welcome any challenges and roles offered. I have enjoyed working with you on previous briefs and print production and would love to work with you again.

From previous work on commissioned projects, I have been allowed enough practice and responsibility to work within a team to give design advice and solutions for a number of different mediums.

I have attached a few nice things I am enjoying from my work at the moment. Thank you for your time.

Yours sincerely,

An informative, friendly, and enthusiastic introduction will keep the reader reading.

Your résumé and portfolio should elaborate on and support such claims.

There is nothing wrong with acknowledging that you have a lot to learn, and are eager to do so.

Dear John Smith

My name is Mina and I have recently graduated from Communication Design at Anytown University.

I am sending you my résumé and work samples. It would be great to have an opportunity to come to your studio and show you my portfolio.

This is my website, where you can look at more of my work www.mina.co.uk

I hope to hear from you soon.

Best regards

◀ Be concise

⭐ All the elements that are needed for a speculative cover letter are here. The student says what she would like to happen, shows some enthusiasm for wanting to meet in person, and provides PDFs of work and a link to further examples online.

Do ⭐

- Keep the cover letter to one page.

- If you are e-mailing the letter, make sure that type size is legible and the letter will open in different formats. You could ask someone else to check on another computer.

- Check then check again for spelling mistakes. It is critical that your cover letter contain no errors. If it does, then you are in danger of not making it past the first stage.

▶ State your purpose

⭐ Be clear on who you are, what you want, and what you have to offer.

Communicate who you are and your intentions in the first sentence.

Computer skills are important, and useful in a busy design studio. However, be sure to mention other skills such as crafts, photography, or printmaking.

Dear John Smith

I am a second year graphic design student and I am looking for work placement. I am mainly interested in design for print and would love to have the opportunity to work with and learn more about Studio Design. The variety of work on the website is intriguing and so I would love to see and know more. I particularly like the exhibition identity. I have good knowledge of such software as Photoshop, Illustrator, and InDesign. I am enthusiastic and hard working, I am always on time and I put my heart into everything I do.

I look forward to hearing from you,

Don't ✖

- Don't assert excellent team skills if in fact you can't prove them.

- Don't overdesign your cover letter. However, do follow the industry standards of good design: that it communicates who you are with typography fit for the purpose.

- Don't exaggerate. Saying "performed extremely well under stress and produced excellent results" when you are referring only to your college education is inappropriate. Avoid saying that you are "exceptionally talented"—this sounds hollow unless you can back it up.

- Don't claim you are highly proficient in a software program if you are not— be truthful about skill levels.

- Don't use abbreviations (such as "pls" for "please," lowercase "i" for "I" and other shorthand common to the language of text messaging.

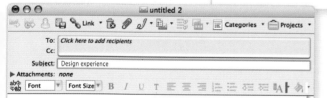

Dear John Smith

My name is Paul Little and I am a recent graduate from The Creative Arts School. Over the next few months, I am trying to acquire some design experience, no matter how big or small. Would you consider taking me on for even a two-week placement (unpaid) in the next couple of months? I'm a hard worker and have a laptop to work on.

I have sent a PDF of some of my work for you to have a look at and a link to my website, so you can make an informed decision.

Many thanks

◀ Show that you understand the company

⭐ This student shows that he understands that it is a big investment of time and resources for small studios to offer work placements. By offering to bring his own laptop, he is providing an easy solution to a small studio that may not have spare workstations.

A basic website or blog of your portfolio is essential if you want to portray yourself as a serious designer.

When to declare disabilities or learning difficulties?

Look to national guidelines for disclosing disabilities. In the United States the relevant organization is www.disability.gov.

Common mistakes in cover letters

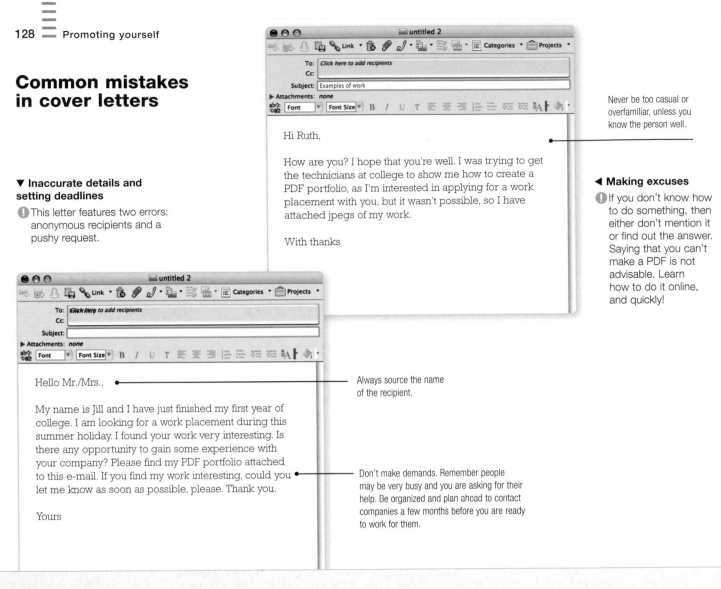

Never be too casual or overfamiliar, unless you know the person well.

▼ Inaccurate details and setting deadlines

❶ This letter features two errors: anonymous recipients and a pushy request.

> Hi Ruth,
>
> How are you? I hope that you're well. I was trying to get the technicians at college to show me how to create a PDF portfolio, as I'm interested in applying for a work placement with you, but it wasn't possible, so I have attached jpegs of my work.
>
> With thanks

◄ Making excuses

❶ If you don't know how to do something, then either don't mention it or find out the answer. Saying that you can't make a PDF is not advisable. Learn how to do it online, and quickly!

> Hello Mr./Mrs.,
>
> My name is Jill and I have just finished my first year of college. I am looking for a work placement during this summer holiday. I found your work very interesting. Is there any opportunity to gain some experience with your company? Please find my PDF portfolio attached to this e-mail. If you find my work interesting, could you let me know as soon as possible, please. Thank you.
>
> Yours

Always source the name of the recipient.

Don't make demands. Remember people may be very busy and you are asking for their help. Be organized and plan ahead to contact companies a few months before you are ready to work for them.

Key terms

Searching for magic terminology in perfect job applications produces many résumés that read as though the same person wrote them. Instead, use the following recommended phrases as a framework within which you can build individual descriptions, but use them with care. You can have your application checked at various career services.

Experience

Demonstrated skills in…
Practical background in…
Experienced as/in aspects of…
Experience included…
Working knowledge of…
Proficient in…
Provided technical assistance to…
Familiar with…

Training

Proficient in/competent at…
Initially employed to…
Expert at…
Knowledge of…
Coordinated…
Organized…

Success

Promoted to…
Succeeded in…
Successful in/at…
Proven track record in…
Instrumental in…
Delivered…

Responsibilities

In charge of…
Supervised/delegated…
Involved in/coordinated…
Employed to/handled…
Assigned to…
Project managed…

Roles

Analyzed/evaluated…
Created/designed…
Initiated…
Managed…
Presented…

Personal attributes

Committed to…
Confident
Enthusiastic
Thorough
Actively sought…

Dear Chris,

I have recently graduated from The Arts Institute and was introduced to your website last week. I am currently in the process of working at as many design studios as possible, where I can soak up experience, and develop my knowledge and passion for design.

Upon viewing your online portfolio I found your collection of work both an inspiration and a pleasure to view. The opportunity to produce conceptual ideas in a refreshing, fun, and professional manner not only excites me, but also inspires me to want to design.

Therefore, I am writing to inquire about the possibility of a work placement with you. I feel I can connect to your way of innovative thinking and pushing an idea out of its boundaries, in order to produce the beautifully unexpected. I am eager to learn and develop the imagination and skills I already process, and feel this would be the perfect opportunity.

Thanking you for your time, and I look forward to hearing from you soon.

◀ **Writing too much**

⚠ Be passionate about what you do, but avoid flowery, confusing language.

A busy art director will not have time to wade through this and work out what you are in fact trying to say. Be clear about what you are looking for and you will have a better chance of getting it.

Don't overdo it: your letter will become disingenuous and fake. Just mention one project that you particularly like.

Don't focus on what you want to learn; save this for the interview. Instead, clearly state what you have to offer.

Following up

After you have contacted someone, it is nerve-wracking wondering if and when they will reply. Many designers are busy and may be seeing lots of other candidates. If you've had an interview, keep in touch by sending a thank-you note, if appropriate. This could be sent via e-mail of course, but refrain from e-mailing every day—you risk looking desperate and becoming a nuisance. Consider sending a relevant postcard for a more original approach—one you picked up at a design exhibition, or, better still, something relevant to a conversation in your interview, perhaps even designed by you, if you have the time.

```
! W I T H C O M P L I M E N T S !
E W H A T T H A T L O O K I N G N
V X A Y R E V N Y O U S S W A E I
A S C S O E E Y O O H T L E M T C
H T W E L L D O N E L H O I X H E
F A B U L O U S R U A E S G J A O
X R L G O O D A T T L O T H O N N
L U V L O V E L Y H A I R T B K E
! Y A Y O U R B E E S K N E E S !
```

Say "thank you"

⭐ This example is a compliment card that doubles as a thank-you card. The letters relevant to the message are highlighted.

Should you brand your cover letter?

If you are into branding and advertising, and it suits your approach, then yes, brand your cover letter. For other fields, if it does not feel appropriate, then keep it simple.

Brighten up

⭐ This lively cover letter is matched with lively text: "Hello, I saw your note (on Blackboard) and I thought this is good!" This tone is appropriate for someone you know through a contact, a network, or a college environment. It is sent as a PDF and a bold use of color oozes confidence, a good quality in a young designer.

Edward Johansson
/ edward@internet.net
/ 0777 022 88888

March 8 2010

Hello
I saw your note on Blackboard and thought, "this is good!"

My name is Edward, I like bicycles, coffee, and type (in alphabetical order as I couldn't decide on a hierarchy). OK, so I'm including a résumé and some work samples, don't hesitate to get in touch if you have any questions. If you want a second opinion my tutor is Karen, I reckon she has me figured out.

I will enclose an extended version of my résumé at the end, after my work samples.

2010–present	school	Central Saint Martins BA Graphic Design
Dec 2009	work placement	April Kommunikation
2009	school	Umeå Universitet History of Photography
2007–08	school	Kulturama Photography

I am available any time between mid-June and mid-September, and for anywhere between three and ten weeks.

Looking forward to hearing from you.

Edward Johansson

Brand your note

⭐ This thank-you letter was sent to everyone who looked at the advertising portfolio featured on pages 64–69. It is graphically striking, friendly, and memorable, the kind of item a designer might keep and pin up on their bulletin board. It came in its own envelope, too.

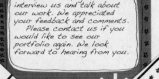

Dear Tim

Thanks for taking the time to interview us and talk about our work. We appreciated your feedback and comments. Please contact us if you would like to see our portfolio again. We look forward to hearing from you.

What to write

⭐ Keep it short and friendly, and convey your appreciation.

Starting your own business

Going freelance or setting up your own studio requires skills and knowledge beyond graphic design. You do need talent, but you shouldn't rely on your artistic capabilities alone.

There are a number of aspects to consider: the capacity to be organized, the ability to communicate well, a degree of self-confidence, the ability to promote your own work, and as for any field in which you have to be self-motivated, discipline. All of this put together represents professionalism. You should also have an idea of your options for earning money—being self- or part-employed, on a temporary contract, and freelancing on-site or from your own office.

Going freelance

Being a freelance designer varies between working on-site—going into a design office—and a second kind of freelancer, where you take the work away and do it at your own studio. Or you may be a remote worker, connected via the Web.

Being self-employed and employed

You can be both self-employed and work for various employers on short-term contracts. It is common practice to be self-employed and employed at the same time. Some designers survive by having a part-time job, say two days a week in a studio, and working freelance around that job.

You should check the self-employment laws in your country and find out your tax position. Check with national design standards guidelines online for advice. Your design network will also help you. Find out who can recommend an accountant for sole traders and small businesses. You must set aside funds to pay the taxes due at the end of each fiscal year.

Designing on-site

In the United States and Europe, if you go into a company and work at a design station on their premises, then you are likely to be treated as being employed, so you will be taxed by the employer at a higher rate than if you took the work back to your design studio. Because of the collaborative nature of designing in publishing, you will often go into the premises even though you are freelance.

Working off-site: outsourcing

Someone who works away from the office is called an outworker. For instance, if you design for the Web, the tax position is different, as you are using your own utilities. A digital outworker can be briefed online and never even visit the premises of the client. As a young designer starting out, you should check with local design support networks, with your tax accountant, and with national design guidelines for the best practice. If you have the benefit of a college alumni association, use their resources too.

Useful websites

The following websites offer plenty of advice and support for freelance graphic designers.

www.spd.org/student-outreach
This is a good place to start.

www.ed2010.com
Excellent advice for magazine designers.

www.aiga.org/content.cfm/get-a-job
For general advice about getting a design job.

www.aiga.org/content.cfm/salary-survey
For salary advice.

www.freelancersunion.org
Advice, forums, and jobs for freelancers.

www.graphicartistsguild.org/handbook
Up-to-date advice on professional practices.

Organization

As a self-employed graphic designer, you'll be working to tight deadlines, juggling several projects at once, and driving your own business. You must be organized.

Effective workspace

It may sound pedantic and boring, but setting up an efficient system early on will give you more time to be creative in the end. A messy workspace never helped any designer be productive.

The best solution is to have a separate studio dedicated solely to your work, but if that's not possible, section off a corner of a room for this purpose. What's really important is to have a desk or a workspace where you can leave work in progress, without having to put everything away at the end of each day. Nothing kills inspiration (and time) like having to set up your workspace every time you start work.

Ideally, you should always aim to finish short/low fee assignments by the end of the day. This isn't always possible, especially when you're just starting out. In the beginning, even smaller jobs will take a few days, and you might have more than one job lying on your desk. So you need a system that allows you to move easily from working on one project to another.

Accessibility

Have your references and inspiration accessible. Sometimes, just getting up to look in a reference book is enough to break your flow and concentration. One tip is to have a bulletin board in front of your desk where you can pin up useful reference pictures and photographs.

At the center of your workspace will be your computer, hooked up to a fast and reliable Internet connection and furnished with all the relevant software. Your computer will also act as your main point of contact to the outside world, so it's worth investing in something up-to-date and more than adequate for your needs, to minimize losing time and money through avoidable technical hitches.

Also make sure that all the materials you need—such as sketchbooks and pencils—are at hand when you start work. Have a little extra of everything in store, so that you don't have to interrupt your work when you run out of paper or toner.

Filing systems

Everyone has a personal way to store information. Just find the one that best suits you. Avoid duplicates and multiple folders. One method is to simply have one folder titled "Commissions," inside which you have a separate file for each agency; then, in each agency file, put your individual job files.

Always archive your work so that when you get called back for a follow-up job, you know exactly where to find the relevant pieces. Sometimes revisions can come up when you've completely forgotten about a job. Use ringbinders and plastic folders to organize your work. Binders are great for organizing old jobs, reference material, and keeping track of invoices.

Time zones

When working with people in other countries, be sure to keep track of the time difference between your location and theirs. Otherwise you might accidentally wake someone up—or, worse still, find that your seven o'clock deadline actually passed six hours ago! Of course, there are also potential benefits, as you may find that the time difference gives you a few extra hours' leeway to finish your job before your colleagues have even made it to the office.

Finances

As a freelancer, you'll be in charge of your own invoices. Keep track of each job you do, noting the date, contact person, company, hours, and, of course, your fee. Make note of when you send in the invoice and when it's due. Send the invoice as soon as the job is completed. You'll be working on several jobs at once, and it's easy to forget.

Negotiate your fee in advance to avoid any misunderstanding. If you're working for a foreign company, find out what the invoicing procedure is in that particular country. It varies. In Italy, for example, the standard due time on an invoice is three to six months!

Pros and cons

⭐ You can be employed and self-employed simultaneously, so part-time work can help you establish yourself.

⭐ A requisite excellent portfolio will inspire confidence. To build this portfolio, you could take a job to gain solid experience of negotiating with clients while under the supervision of a studio.

⭐ By keeping expenses to a minimum, you can start up in lean economic times and have little to lose. However, if you are the type to be distracted by buying tools and would rather do that than meet clients, then you are a nonstarter.

❗ You need to be able to network, be confident about approaching people, and follow up every single lead to yield paid jobs.

❗ Tax and insurance requirements are greater for self-employment than for employment.

❗ Isolation can be an issue. Build up a network of contacts and support systems well before starting a business. See local business advice for the design industry, and check the AIGA website (www.aiga.org).

Searching for jobs

No matter how accomplished your portfolio, you must first determine where you want to be and then meet the right people to show them your work. This section examines how to contact potential employers.

Before you embark on the process of finding the right job, ask yourself these questions: What kind of job am I looking for? Do I want to be freelance or get a permanent position? What kind of environment is best for me? Would I prefer a large team or a small studio? What are my strengths and weaknesses?

Consider your ideal job and discuss answers with a friend who can help reflect on your working style. The point of this exercise in self-knowledge is not to consider a possible choice of offers, but to prevent wasting time and energy. Finding the right job can take time; it won't happen overnight. Expect a number of interviews without being successful. Treat this process as a series of steps in the right direction. Try to enjoy the journey—with each experience you learn a little more about where you want to be and the kind of designers you feel at home with.

Know the industry

It is vital that you find out about your chosen design field. Research it by examining design annuals in arts libraries and looking up websites of companies that interest you. Employers may even publish a mission statement that will give you an idea of their world view. Attend lectures and events based around this industry. Participate if you can in conferences and online communities. Try to meet other designers in the business and then ask them intelligent questions about how they got started. Find out their tips to help you to get a foot in the door.

Word of mouth and personal contacts are the widely used means to find new people. Designers often ask their friends, "Do you know any students or have you seen anyone talented lately?" There are few job advertisements— many agencies don't want to spend the money, so few positions are filled this way.

Build a support community

Talk to people and gather contacts. Surround yourself with friends and other designers in the field. Support them; they can offer you support in return. Go with a friend to industry events if you feel uncomfortable going alone. If you have the benefit of a college education, use the final year to set yourself up for the job search ahead. Stay in touch, ask for advice, meet, show each other portfolios. A support network helps after rejection: Friends will remind you that it happens to everyone and is just part of the journey. Pick yourself up and carry on.

Beyond your own group you will need to contact people in the industry. Meeting them can be nerve-wracking, but designers are generally nice people who like to communicate. They are rarely hierarchical and have all been in your position. On gaining contacts, talk to them and be normal. Don't push too hard or be desperate—your preparation and portfolio should instill the confidence to just be yourself.

So you didn't go to college

Not everyone has the opportunity or means to get a college education, but you may have natural talent and be prepared to create your own portfolio. In fact, many designers are self-taught, so don't let a lack of opportunity put you off.

One fear is that workplace conversation during coffee break may start with, "So what did you do at college?" If you can afford to get any kind of college tuition, even short courses or evening courses, this will give you more confidence in the workplace. All designers have to work hard to keep up-to-date with both software and design trends.

How to meet other designers

• Go to industry events, lectures, and conferences. Volunteer with design organizations—they often need assistants for events.

• Join an organization as a student and attend events. Talk to people—don't be afraid to introduce yourself. Here you can talk informally, as you will have some common ground.

• Inform your teachers of what you are looking for in case they hear of anything. Some alumni groups are useful, although you may find it more constructive to stick to designer groups.

• Join a designer community that shares studio space or is in an informal support group. Such groups are becoming increasingly popular, so you shouldn't have too much difficulty finding one.

• Be brave: At social events, ask the host to introduce you to other designers.

• Contact designers you have heard speak and tell them you appreciated their talk. Write to a magazine art director and say you liked the last issue. Send a postcard to say how you admired a book design. You will be surprised at how few people make direct contact in this way.

Changing fields

Switching fields is possible though not easy. This is a flexible industry, and if you can show an interest in one area, you will find people willing to give you a chance. You can often build on knowledge from similar professions. For instance, fine artists often bring a boldness to graphic design work, and spatial designers often reveal a great sense of form and color.

• Study design thinking and approaches. Graphics is not just learning software; it is also learning how to think about communication at a deeper level, before you even start on surface design.

• If you have tried book design for a couple of years but want something different, decide first whether the company or the field itself is the problem. Research other companies and approach them directly.

• If you feel like a clean break, start building a portfolio. First, think about a chosen route and try to get into the appropriate mind-set. For example, if considering brand design (see page 52), then try to think like a brand designer or even brand manager. Then structure work around this approach. Fill any gaps in your portfolio by setting yourself a brief or by redesigning an existing brand.

• Look for appointments, not for a job but to seek advice about your portfolio. E-mail work or send it in, and follow up with a phone call. If you have any contacts or friends in the new field, ask their opinion and see if they can give you a contact to approach.

The interview process

With sufficient preparation and a few points to remember, an interview is your chance to flaunt your assets and prove you are the one for the job.

The secret of a successful interview is in the preparation. If you arrive well prepared and informed, you will be relaxed and confident. Research will put you in good stead for whatever happens next.

Before

• Find out directions beforehand. Aim to arrive fifteen minutes early. If you are going to an unfamiliar area, bring a map to make sure you don't get lost. Always be on time.

• Take a pen and notebook for any names or Web references you are given. Bring any letters about the position or the company. If you are going to a recruitment agency, read the terms and conditions beforehand so you can ask intelligent questions.

• Research studio output, both the kind of work and the work on the site. Knowing the company size will help gauge the type of interview. If there are fewer than five people, it will probably be relaxed and open. Other people may walk by and look at your portfolio too, so enjoy this chance for communication. Larger agencies may hold interviews in someone's workspace or in a meeting room.

• Take a copy of your résumé. Keep it up-to-date and remember what it contains—an interviewer could ask about a particular detail. Always own up to group work, especially if your work was credited in a competition.

During

• You have the first ten seconds to make a good impression: Shake hands, make eye contact, and pay attention to your body language—keep both feet flat on the floor and uncrossed, relax your shoulders, face the interviewer, smile, and speak clearly and at an appropriate pace and volume.

• Don't worry about interview panels—these are not standard platforms in the design business except for more senior positions with responsibilities. If it is a formal panel situation, such as for a teaching position at a design school, you will be informed beforehand to ensure fair play. You won't be expected to give any kind of presentation unless that is specified in a letter inviting you for an interview.

• When is the right time to talk about salary? This depends on the situation. In a meeting as a "go see" for advice on your portfolio, there probably isn't a job offer. Here you can talk generally at the end about the starting salary for a junior designer. In an interview for a specific vacancy, the salary range will have been declared, but the aim in the interview is to establish where you fit within that range. You can ask the hypothetical question, "If you were to hire someone from the candidates on offer, what would the salary be?"

• Prepare a few questions for the interviewer, as most interviews end with, "Do you have any questions for us about the job?" You can ask about opportunities within the company, or other issues related to the ad. Prepare more than one in case your question is answered during the course of the interview.

Top questions to ask

"How many candidates are on the short-list?"

"Will you be able to let me know soon if I have been successful?"

"When will you let me know the salary range—now or at a later stage?"

"Do you have any constructive feedback?"

Questions to avoid

"What does your company do?" You should have researched this.

"When can I start?" Don't be so bold.

"Can I get more money than the advertised salary?" This is unlikely.

Questions you might be asked

"Where is your real strength? Design or project managing?"

"Have you ever had to adapt a design at the request of someone else (a client, an instructor)? Was it better or worse as a result?"

"What did you leave out of your portfolio today, and why?"

"What's the most impressive piece of design you have seen this year? What has least impressed you?"

"Compare these designs of logos/pages/jackets: which works best, and why?"

Tips for video interviews

For Web skills in particular, you might find yourself working for clients in different countries. Most of these jobs are done on a freelance, project-by-project basis and do not involve a lengthy employment contract, but the company may still want to have a good idea of who they are working with, so it is possible you will be asked to take part in an online interview, through a video-call program such as Skype.

Prepare beforehand as for other interviews. Research the company and find out the name and role of the interviewer.

Prepare your home office or studio so that background items are not distracting.

Consider body language. Position yourself center-screen. Make sure lighting is suitable and your face is not in shadow. Use eye contact—speak directly and clearly into the screen. Interviewers are looking for communication skills, to see if they could talk to you, especially if you speak a different language or are a continent away. Leave sufficient pauses so that you can hear what they have to say.

At the end, ask any questions, thank interviewers for their time, and send contact details. If you want to look back on how you performed, record the conversation on your computer for later review.

Appropriate attire

Don't overdress so that you are uncomfortable. Unlike typical office work, you don't need a business suit or heels. Research what other designers wear. The best advice is to look smart, as if you were going to a private viewing or upscale restaurant and didn't want to look out of place.

Don't underdress either. Avoid anything extreme, and definitely don't wear anything dirty, no matter how trendy disheveled or ripped clothing may be. The design field has a level of individuality in dress—such creativity is welcome, but don't overdo it on a first meeting. Most designers specify "smart casual."

Afterward

Ask for feedback. In a formal situation, interviewers may keep notes. In an informal scenario, you can ask less for direct critique than for tips on how to improve your portfolio or general presentation.

Follow up every interview with a thank-you note or e-mail. If you are unsuccessful, an e-mail is an opportunity to ask for feedback on how to improve. Asking why you didn't get the job is a bit too direct.

Reflect on how you did. Talk it over with a friend and note what you could do better next time. Don't be disappointed if you were unsuccessful; remember even top designers have been knocked back at some point, and they just keep on going.

Learn from each experience. You will look back on some of your mistakes later and laugh. Not every agency will be right for you; some interviews can be quite enjoyable, a chance to look around and get a feel for a place. For example, you might prefer the environment of an informal bustling studio over a quiet, intense agency.

How to survive an internship

Here is some advice from two recent graduates, Danni and Nat, who have been through the process of finding and working internships.

⭐ Introduce yourself on the first day. Circulate an e-mail or go personally around the office and say "Hi." If you don't, no one will bother to get to know you—make sure people know you are there. When work is short, improve your portfolio, and cram in as many reviews as possible early on. These are great ways to meet people and get help.

⭐ Find out who clients are, take the initiative, and work for them without a brief if you have no work. Find out who group heads are on accounts and show them your ideas—you'll look very proactive.

⭐ Be sociable. If you are invited to an event, go; if you hear of an event, ask about tickets, as some people may not go. Make as many contacts as possible. Talk to people and remember them so you can talk more informatively next time.

⭐ Be nice to everyone, especially personal assistants and receptionists. Always be nice to computer people. You never know when or how someone could help you. Be polite, not arrogant—people may seem arrogant to you but are probably just shy like all of us.

⭐ Be enthusiastic about every brief; don't turn your nose up at something that sounds boring. It is harder to do an inspired ad for something mundane than for a well-known product—you'll get more respect.

⭐ Be prepared to take a paid job to fund your internship.

Promotional ideas

Once you have finished preparation and your portfolio is ready, what next? To conduct a job search and build up a network you need to promote yourself. This section studies how designers set themselves apart using graphic design skills.

Unique skills in self-promotion

Designers can transcend the standard remit of résumé and cover letter to create specially targeted items. The most common tools are business cards and calling cards—simple pieces of communication including contact details. Unique solutions below show how a little imagination can go a long way.

Specially targeted items

The most labor-intensive items are one-off promotional pieces aimed at a few people or particular agency. These are expensive to produce but can make an impact.

◄ Aim for specific people

✪ This lavish promotion was aimed at three creatives in an ad agency and succeeds in making a powerful impression. The yellow band is a clever device for naming the three people. For another interview, a different band could easily be tailor-made.

► Copywriting skills

✪ This statement of intent is an excellent example of copywriting. Instead of using a résumé for a personal statement, this candidate has designed it and made it vibrant.

I AM TOTALLY EXCITED. I AM ON AN ADVENTURE. I DON'T KNOW WHERE I AM GOING TO END UP BUT I KNOW WHICH DIRECTION I AM GOING IN. I WANT TO BE ONE OF THE BEST CREATIVES IN THE WORLD, EARN LOTS OF MONEY, HAVE SO MANY SHOES I CAN'T FIND A MATCHING PAIR AND HAVE APPARTMENTS IN LONDON, NEW YORK, BERLIN AND GATESHEAD. I AM BEING HONEST. LAST YEAR ON THE 8TH OCTOBER I WROTE OUT A ONE MILLION POUND CHEQUE TO MYSELF. ONE DAY I WILL CASH IT. IN THE LAST DECADE I HAVE BEEN PREPARING MYSELF FOR THIS GRAND ADVENTURE. I HAVE FIGURED OUT WHAT IT IS A CREATIVE DOES AND NOW I AM READY TO GO. TO BE ONE OF THE BEST CREATIVES IN THE WORLD I HAVE TO START AT ONE OF THE BEST AGENCIES IN THE WORLD. THERE IS NO REASON WHY THIS IS NOT POSSIBLE. I CAN'T SOAR LIKE AN EAGLE SURROUNDED BY A BUNCH OF TURKEYS.

Lauranda Reid
itslauranda@
00 49 163 478 0

I HAVE SPOKEN.

◄ Direct messages

✪ The back page of this booklet has a simple head shot and contact details. This powerful and compelling message is perfect for targeting an ad agency.

▼ Strong messages

✪ The A5 book continues with this strong message ("Gis a job" is slang for "Give me a job"). Pages are designed like a magazine with a double-page spread as a canvas.

▼ Maximize the format

✪ The urgent message of this A5 book is dramatic and visual, and so would be successful in targeting an advertising agency. The typography is bold and changes scale to reflect variety in the delivery of the message.

I WANT TO BE HERD

Ceci n'est pas une baignoire

GIS JOB
Please.

▲ Impress with finish

⭐ This item impresses with a high level of finish. The book, wittily titled *A Gentleman's Guide to a Successful Placement*, is printed and hand-bound by the graduate and is a complete piece—idea and format as one.

▲ Witty design

⭐ This hand-bound booklet for an internship application is a clever pastiche of an etiquette guide, popular in the early twentieth century. Text continually references smart links between etiquette tips and work in a general design studio.

▼ Target marketing

⭐ This book features a play on words, making clever reference on the first page (in the form of a school prize-day label) to the target agency as the prizewinner, and the applicant as the awarder of the prize.

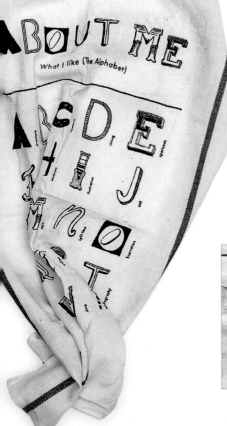

◄ Make it memorable

⭐ Printed on high-quality linen, this tea towel has quirky drawn typography with the memorable message "About Me, What I like (The Alphabet)."

❗ There are many giveaway items you could use, some very cheap and gimmicky, so beware.

▼ Simple communication

⭐ Detail includes the student's name printed on the label— an understated yet really effective method of communication.

► Be one step ahead

⭐ Network to get your message across. The student, a cloakroom volunteer at a magazine design social event, dropped a card into each coat so that the wearer discovered the message "I looked after your coat in the cloakroom at the party—I did a good job didn't I?…I'm quite good at graphic design too. If you give me a ring I'll come and show you my work or I'll send you my CV…" The message is gently persuasive.

◄ Opportune networking

⭐ Another example from a cloakroom volunteer, this dry-cleaning ticket was pinned to each coat with the witty line "Damn good dry cleaning and design." The torn edges and hand-numbered design give an authentic feel, and the message is humorous.

Promotional cards

Clever ideas are liked universally. No one wants a dull card—it will end up in the trash. These small and postcard-size cards show how to make an impact.

▲ Wordplay

⭐ Student Gabrielle Sharp used a picture of a "Sharpie" (the famous marker pen) as a simple solution for instant recall of her name.

▼ Ready to work

⭐ Graduation is a chance for self-promotion and a bit of fun. This graduate's tongue-in-cheek card, announcing herself as "Design Soldier," emphasizes that she is keen to work.

◀ Talent-spotting tricks

⭐ This card was given out as a witty joke by a young team: "You have been spotted by them—innovative design team, Anthony and Ingrid." The idea is one of reversal. They like you so they give you the card. Clever twists stick in the mind of those often approached in more conventional ways.

John Balsom

▲ Double-sided cards

⭐ This photographer's double-sided card gives maximum exposure. The photos are colorful and the locations unusual, and his Web address is written discreetly along the bottom edge.

◀ Embossed card

⭐ In a high-tech world, a nicely printed card on cartridge paper is a treat. Traditional crafts like letterpress feel nice in the hand. Here embossed letterforms imply crispness and efficiency. Such finishing techniques are undergoing a revival. They were overused in the 1980s, but, like fashion, they return when a new generation discovers them.

◀ Simple typography

⭐ If typography is your forté, look no farther. This freelancer's card is a sure way to affirm intentions for employment. Keep it simple.

▲ Hand-printed luxury

⭐ Here the student used just her name and circles to produce simple silk-screened one-off cards.

▼ Straight-talking lonely heart

⭐ This student used the visual language of the lonely-hearts ad: "Talented, good looking designer seeks employment," an appealing and lighthearted message.

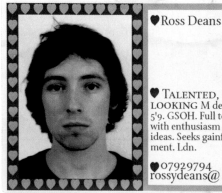

♥Ross Deans

♥ TALENTED, GOOD LOOKING M designer, 20's, 5'9. GSOH. Full to the brim with enthusiasm and original ideas. Seeks gainful employment. Ldn.

♥07929794
rossydeans@

◀ Watch your briefs!

⭐ This still-life photograph shows that the simplest of images can be eye-catching. The postcard reflects attention to detail in ordinary everyday items. The photographer's name is on the reverse, leaving the image plain.

Do ⭐

- Use something that reflects your style. Avoid anything that doesn't fit your personality, no matter how impressive it looks.

- Keep cards with you at all times and give them out to friends and family too.

- Change your card whenever you like. You will keep remaking your brands so keep updating your card.

▶ Use striking images

✴ An invitation to an MA show doubles as a photographer's card, using bold cropping with mismatched pupils. Text says, "You won't like everything…but you will love some things" and the reverse connects the image to the idea "As you'll see, these were never ordinary pupils." This is the kind of card that people keep and pin on a bulletin board.

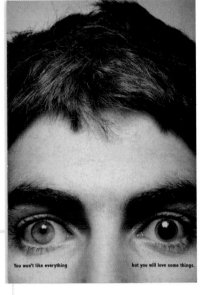

You won't like everything   but you will love some things.

Don't ✖

- Don't use the cheapest card in the print shop. This is not for graphic designers. Take the time and trouble to represent yourself properly.

- Don't forget to include your name and contact details clearly. I have seen great designs but without a name.

- Don't copy any of the examples shown here. Use them for inspiration but create your own idea. Start with something simple.

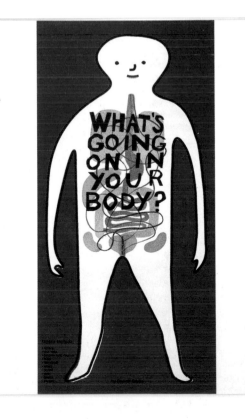

WHAT'S GOING ON IN YOUR BODY?

◀ Think it through

⭐ If you are using a sample, make sure you choose wisely. This silk-screened image of the body still has impact when reduced to card size.

▶ Make it interesting

⭐ This MA student investigated type in depth and used cross-stitch in her final exhibition. She photographed the work for her printed card instead of stitching every one.

Printed Matter   Evelin Kasikov
An experiment   evelin.kasikov@
in craft and design   + 44 (0) 79 5646 3

Resources

Here are some useful suggestions for sources of inspiration for your work and career. Some apply only to certain continents and/or countries, but all provide further information and a steppingstone toward helping you to improve your knowledge and prospects.

Organizations

Advertising Age
www.adage.com
Advertising and marketing
industry news.

The Art Directors Club (ADC)
www.adcglobal.org
A self-funding, not-for-profit membership organization whose mission is to connect, provoke, and elevate creative visual communications professionals around the world.

American Institute of Graphic Arts
www.aiga.org
The oldest and largest professional membership organization for design.

Association Typographique Internationale
www.atypi.org
Global forum and focal point for the type community and business.

Design and Art Direction
www.dandad.org
UK-based charitable organization that runs prestigious Global Awards.

Society of Illustrators
www.societyillustrators.org
Promotes illustration through exhibitions, lectures, and education.

Society of Graphic Designers of Canada
www.gdc.net
National certified body of graphic designers promoting high standards of visual design and ethical business practices.

Type Directors Club
www.tdc.org
International organization that supports excellence in typography, both in print and on screen.

The Society of Publication Designers
www.spd.org
Promotes and encourages excellence in editorial design.

Magazines

Communication Arts
www.commarts.com
Source of inspiration for anyone involved in visual communication.

Design Week
www.designweek.co.uk
Graphics, digital, interior, print, retail, and design news and jobs.

Eye Magazine
www.eyemagazine.com/home.php
International review of graphic design.

HOW Design
www.howdesign.com
Magazine that includes business information, technological tips, the creative reasoning and background to leading projects, and profiles of influential graphic-design professionals.

i-D
www.i-dmagazine.com
Contemporary style guide including collections, art, print, design, music reviews, and interviews.

The International Design Magazine (I.D.)
www.id-mag.com
All the latest developments and cutting-edge projects from the design industry.

Print Magazine
www.printmag.com
Bimonthly magazine about visual culture and design. Covers commercial, social, and environmental design.

Education

Parsons The New School for Design, New York
www.newschool.edu/parsons

Graphic Art School, School of Visual Arts, New York
www.schoolofvisualarts.edu

Central Saint Martins, London University of the Arts
www.csm.arts.ac.uk

Books

Graphic Design Theory

Fletcher, Alan, *The Art of Looking Sideways,* Phaidon Press, 2001
McAlhone and Stuart, *A Smile in the Mind: Witty Thinking in Graphic Design,* Phaidon Press, 1998
Olins, Wally, *Wally Olins on Brand,* Thames & Hudson, 2003
Rand, Paul, *Thoughts on Design,* Littlehampton Book Services Ltd, 1970
Stevens, Andrew, *Graphic Thought Facility (GTF): Bits World (Directions),* Capelli, 2003

Typography

Baines and Haslam, *Type & Typography,* Laurence King, 2005
Birdsall, Derek, *Notes on Book Design,* Yale University Press, 2004
Lupton, Ellen, *Thinking with Type,* Princeton Architectural Press, 2004

Careers in Design

Barringer, David, *There's Nothing Funny About Design,* Princeton Architectural Press, 2009
Heller, Steven, *Becoming a Graphic Designer: A Guide to Careers in Design,* Wiley, 2005
Lupton, Ellen, *DIY: Design it Yourself,* Princeton Architectural Press, 2005
Millman, Debbie, *How to Think Like a Great Graphic Designer,* Allworth Press, 2008
Shaughnessy, Adrian, *How to Be a Graphic Designer: Without Losing Your Soul,* Laurence King, 2005

ISO A series

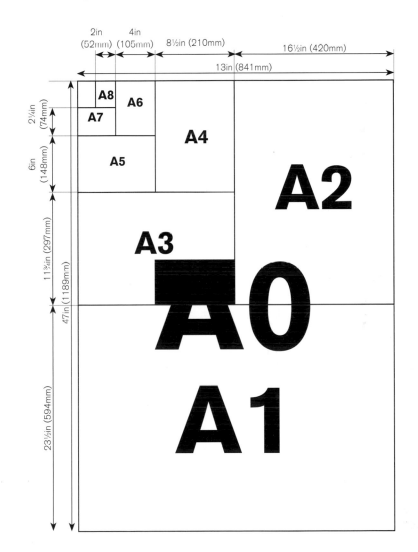

Index

A

academic level 13
Adobe Dreamweaver 104, 115
advertising agency 62–71
  best practice tips 70
  building portfolio for 66–9
  digital portfolio 70–1
  dos and don'ts 65
  first impressions for 64–5
  key skills for 62–3
  pros and cons 63
  work of 63
ambient campaign 67
archive box, carrying 74
art-directing 68
  showing skills at 83
award-winning work 42, 56, 60

B

Behance 110, 117
  case study 112–13
binders, ring-bound 19
blog 106–9
  building 108–9
  case study 107
  comparison with other formats 95
  considerations 108
  essential points 106
  pros and cons 106
book design 72–81
  building portfolio for 76–9
  digital portfolio 80–1
  first impressions for 74–5
  key skills for 72–3
  pros and cons 73
book designers, work of 73
books
  artwork 77
  combining text and images 77
  covers
    creative 72
    information in 76
    series 88
    typography 77
  illustrated 73
brand design agencies 52–61
  building portfolio for 56–9
  digital portfolio 60–1
  dos and don'ts 55
  first impressions for 54–5
  key skills for 52–3
  pros and cons 52
  work of 52
branding, understanding processes 53

business
  organization 131
  pros and cons 131
  starting up 130–1
business cards 26

C

campaigns
  ambient 67
  designing for 62–3
captions 13, 78, 84, 87
Carbonmade 115
CDs 54
character, showing 23
cohesive elements 65
college, not going to 89, 132
color
  flashes of 36
  using 51, 75, 76, 77
color awareness 27
competitions
  awards 42, 60
  briefs 48, 51
  entries 36, 79
contact details, digital 40
copyright statement 104
copywriting, showing skills in 66
cover letter 120
  branding 126, 129
  common mistakes 128
  dos and don'ts 127
  first impressions 126
  following up 129
  key terms 128
  replying to job ad 126
  sending on spec 126
  writing 126–9
creative skills 63
creative thinking 43, 69
creativity 22
credits 56, 87

D

design agency 22–31
  building portfolio for 26–9
  digital portfolio 30–1
  dos and don'ts 25
  first impressions for 24–5
  key skills for 22–3
  pros and cons 22
  work of 22
design studio 32–41
  building portfolio for 36–9
  digital portfolio 40–1
  dos and don'ts 35

first impressions for 34–5
key skills for 32–3
pros and cons 32
work of 32
designers, meeting 133
Deviantart 110, 111
digital format
  print vs. 16–17
  showing knowledge of 53
digital portfolio 94–101, 107
  for advertising agency 70–1
  blog 95
  for book design 80–1
  for brand design 60–1
  building 100–1
  contact details 100
  content-less links 100
  for design agency 30–1
  for design studio 40–1
  dos and don'ts 95, 101
  essential pages 100
  first impressions 96–7
  format comparison 95
  loading speed 96
  logo 97
  for magazine design 90–1
  name presentation 97
  network 95
  for packaging design 50–1
  pros and cons 94
  screen size 96
  scrolling down 30
  showcasing work 98
  sign-posting 96
  site navigation 81, 98–9
  tagline 97
  website 95, 102–5
disabilities, declaring 127
divider pages 15, 37
D.I.Y.: Design It Yourself 89
domain name, choosing 97
drawing, with software 53
drop-off 16
dummy copy 83

E

experimental work 38

F

fields, changing 133
filing systems 131
finances, for self-employed 131
first impressions 14
Flickr 113
fonts 13

first impressions for 34–5
key skills for 32–3
pros and cons 32
work of 32

format 18–19
  experimenting with 87
freelance
  finances 131
  organization 131
  pros and cons 131
  showing work 47, 51, 55
  websites for 130
  working as 130

G

graphics, strong 23
grids
  knowledge of 76
  working with 86–7

H

headers 13
high-impact content 62
humor 68, 79

I

ideas
  development 69
  immediacy of 62
  stealing 69
ideas books 64
identity 88
illustration, incorporating 27
industry awareness 48
information design 38
interactivity
  in print 68
  inviting 74
  using laptop 64
internship
  labeling work from 68
  surviving 135
interviews 134–5
  attire for 135
  questions 134–5

J

jobs
  replying to ads 126
  searching for 132–3
Joomla
  pros and cons 109

L

labeling 64
laptop, showing work on 64
layouts 28, 58, 72
  samples of 83
learning difficulties, declaring 127

letterheads 26, 79
Linkedin 113, 117
logos 57, 97
long-lasting design 23
Lupton, Ellen 89

M

magazine design
 building portfolio for 86–9
 digital portfolio 90–1
 dos and don'ts 85
 first impressions for 84–5
 key skills for 82–3
 portfolio for 82–91
 pros and cons 83
magazine designers, work of 83
magazines, passion for 82
Microsoft Expression Web 104, 115
mock-ups 48, 86
motivation, showing 23
mounts 12
MySpace 113

N

name, placing on portfolio 15
network 110–13
 building 110–11
 case study 112–13
 comparison with other formats 95
 dos and don'ts 111
 pros and cons 110
networking, for self-promotion 137

O

off-site work 130
on-site work 130
online promotion 92–117
 blog 106–9
 domain name 97
 getting noticed 116
 network 110–13
 portfolio 94–101
 single-page site 117
 website 102–5
opening pages 14
originality 33
outworkers 130

P

packaging 15
 understanding 43
packaging design agency 42–51
 building portfolio for 46–9
 digital portfolio 50–1
 dos and don'ts 45

first impressions for 44–5
 key skills for 42–3
 pros and cons 43
 work of 43
packing 14, 19
personal statement 120, 122
Photoshop, re-creating effects of 79
planning 12–15
portfolios
 blog 106–9
 building
  for advertising agency 66–9
  for book design 76–9
  for brand design 56–9
  by self-taught 89
  for design agency 26–9
  for design studio 36–9
  for magazine design 86–9
  online 100–1
  for packaging design 46–9
 editing 20–91
 getting noticed 116
 naming 15
 network 110–13
 online 94–101
 online creators 115
 perfect, pointers for 8–9
 planning 12–15
 preparation 10–19
 size 18–19
 starting 26
 templates 114–15
 website 102–5
preparation 10–19
presentation, keeping tidy 12
print, digital vs. 16–17
production values 27
professional level 13
promotion
 online 92–117
 self- 118–39
  ideas for 136–9
promotional cards 138–9
 dos and don'ts 139
publishing, knowledge of 82

R

referees 120
reference letter 120
research
 sharing 51
 showing skills in 35
résumé 120–5
 clarity 125
 designing 123–5

dos and don'ts 122
 fonts for 123
 information from 70
 keeping up-to-date 125
 personal statement 120, 122
 writing 120–2
ring-bound binders 19

S

search engines 116
self-employment 130
 organization 131
 pros and cons 131
self-publishing 82
self-taught, building portfolio 89
services, advertising 67
shape 18–19
signage 15
size 18–19
sketchbooks 45, 49, 51, 59, 64
software
 drawing with 53
 website-creation 104, 115
spatial awareness 42
staying power 52, 63
support community, building 132

T

taglines 97
tags 13, 84
talking point, creating 34
team players 33
teamwork, crediting 56
Template Monster 115
templates 114–15
 designing 114
 dos and don'ts 115
 finding 114
text, legibility 13
texture, using 75
ThemeForest 114
3-D, projects shown in 41
tidiness 12
time zones, keeping track of 131
Tumblr, pros and cons 109
typography 13
 showing knowledge of 86
 showing love of 72
 showing skills in 25
 type as image 78

V

variety, offering 54
video, uploading 113

W

website 102–5
 building 102–3
 case study 104–5
 comparison with other formats 95
 crucial criteria 105
 domain name 97
 dos and don'ts 103
 pros and cons 105
 templates 114–15
 useful, for freelance 130
witty design 137
WordPress, pros and cons 108
work placement projects 89
workspace 131

Credits

STUDENTS

I need to thank a team of creative students, who offered to share their work with you. They are all associated in some way past and present with Central Saint Martins College of Art and Design, London's largest art and design institution at the University of the Arts, London, UK. Meet us at /my.arts.ac.uk/CSM

PEOPLE

Thanks to my teaching colleagues at Central Saint Martins: Emily Wood, Ruth Sykes, Maggie Gallagher, Yann Jones, and Marc Wood, who offered you their good advice.

There would be no book without the graduates' work: Ed Cornish, Oliver Mayes, Danni Emery and Nat Turton, Michael Kosmicki, Romchat Sangkavatana, Jamie Hearn, and Anders Godal, who all let us into their portfolios.

Thanks to the following professional advisors for their tips to get you started on your professional journey: Tim Leahy and Katy Buck at Leahy Brand Designs; Kath Tudball and Julia Woollams at johnson banks;. ex-graduates now at REG DESIGN, Emily Wood and Ruth Sykes; Katie Crous and Jackie Palmer at Quarto. Moral support supplied by John, Sam, Ed, and Daisy Belknap.

CONTENT

This book depends on the expert support from Chris Jones, who supplied all the content for Chapter 3: Design for Online Promotion.

Thanks to graduates Natalie and Danielle for providing the text for the Do's and Don'ts panel on page 65 and the Survive an Internship sidebar on page 135.

On the cover: Saleem Ahenkora, thanks for your patience!

Key terms panel, page 120. Source: www.prospects. ac.uk

For more advice from the University of the Arts see Creative Living at http://www.careers-creative-living. co.uk/

PAGE CREDITS

Quarto would like to thank the following students, designers, and agencies for kindly supplying images for inclusion in this book:
t = top; m = middle; b = bottom; l = left; r = right

p.2tl, 12b, 139bl Anders Godal www.andersgodal.com
p.2tm, 52, 53t/b Raphael Dominique Wood-Fouchard
p.2tr, 139bl Darrell Gibbs www.sukie.co.uk
p.2bl, 3tm, 15t/m, 18b Oliver Mayes www.olivermayes.co.uk
p.2bm, 43t Monika Koziol http://monikaandfelix.com
p.2br, 82tl/r Cai and Kyn Taylor www.caiandkyn.co.uk

p.3tl, 19br, 22b Reg Design www.regdesign.co.uk
p.3tr Ed Cornish www.edcornish.com
p.3bl, 13m, 15b Romchat Sangkavatana www.romchats.com
p.3bm, 23t, 73b Jean Jullien www.jeanjullien.com
p.8t, 14t, 23bl, 33bl, 104 Jamie Hearn www.jamiehearn.com
p.11t, 12m, 42t, 43b, 49tr Jessica MacDonald
p.12t Lauren Michelle Pires
p.13b, 14bl, 129br Danni Emery and Natalie Turton
p.13t, p17bl Carla Valdivia
p.14br, 33tl Samantha Dunn
p.14bm, 19tl Cherry Tong Wing Yan
p.16tr, 73t Dominic Mylroie
p.16bl Felix Ackermann and Monika Koziol http://monikaandfelix.com
p.17t, 22t Design by Monika Koziol and Felix Ackermann http://monikaandfelix.com; illustration by Kristopher Chun Yat Ho www.kristopherh.com; movie by Tim Keeling http://portfolio.timkeeling.com
p.17br, 19tm, 53m Saleem Ahenkora
p.18t, p.83t/m Andreas Christie Ryalen
p.19bl Ariane Leblanc
p.24–31 Reg Design www.regdesign.co.uk
p.32t, 72tl/b Louise Moe-Dean
p.32b, 33tr/bl, 102 Thomas Yau www.thomasyau.com
p.33tm, 82bl/r Kota Abe
p.34–41 Oliver Mayes www.olivermayes.co.uk
p.42b Nia Murphy and Jessica MacDonald
p.44–51 Romchat Sangkavatana www.romchats.com
p.54–61 Anders Godal www.andersgodal.com
p.56b Anders Godal and Martin Batt
p.62t Ashton Thornton
p.62b Mandy Smith
p.63t Sophie Barker and Kayleigh Brooks
p.64–71 Danni Emery and Natalie Turton
p.72tr/m Michael Kosmicki www.studio-subsist.com
p.74–81 Ed Cornish www.edcornish.com
p.78tr Ed Cornish, Ghaazal Vojdani, Houman Momtazian, and Alex Prior
p.79bl Ed Cornish and Henry Hadlow
p.83b Nuno Miguel Coelho Santos, photos by Marcus Bastel www.marcusbastel.com
p.84–91 Michael Kosmicki www.studio-subsist.com
p.96 Kev Adamson www.kevadamson.com
p.97t Marc Atkinson www.marcalexatkinson.co.uk
p.97m Hannah Warren www.hannahwarren.com
p.97b Ann-Kristina Simon www.duk-duk.com
p.98t Georges Moanack www.g-moanack.com
p.99t Marc Mendell www.marcsdesign.com
p.98-99b Oskar Kron Design www.oskarkron.com
p.100 Hana Stevenson www.hanastevenson.com
p.101t Jamie Gregory www.jamiegregory.co.uk
p.101b Polly Playford www.pollyplayford.com
p.103 Marcus Bastel www.marcusbastel.com

p.106 Tina Roth Eisenberg, Swissmiss www.swiss-miss.com
p.107t Kerry Nehil www.kerrynehil.com
p.107b John "Keebs" Lee www.crackpixels.com
p.117 Isablah www.isablah.com
p.119, 126t Kath Tudball and Julia Woollams
p.121 Helen Altoungarian
p.123t Mike Andrews
p.123b Jimmy Tilley
p.124 Tim Lane
p.125 Margot Bowman
p.129t John Belknap
p.129bl Edward Johansson www.edwardjohansson.com
p.133 Lucy Verrechia
p.136 Lauuranda Reid
p.137t Michael Thompson www.michael-t.co.uk
p.137bl Lottie Whittaker
p.137br Maria Spann
p.137bm Victoria Principal
p.138tl Anthony Webb
p.138tr John Balsom
p.138ml Gabrielle Sharp
p.138m David Lee
p.138mr Anna Keogh
p.138bl Pilar Santos
p.138bm Ned Campbell
p.138br Ross Deans
p.139t Kate Plumb
p.139m Produced by students at the Royal College of Art
p.139br Evelin Kasikov http://evelinkasikov.com

Quarto would also like to thank the following:
http://wordpress.org
www.joomla.org
www.fercadaques.com
www.stephendcookephotography.com
www.tumblr.com
http://graphiceverywhere.tumblr.com
http://itsdesigned.tumblr.com
www.behance.net
www.deviantart.com
www.youtube.com
www.vimeo.com
http://themeforest.net
www.templatemonster.com